COSMO girl!
total body workout
fun moves to look and feel your best

COSMO girl!

total body workout

fun moves to look and feel your best

From the Editors of CosmoGIRL!

HEARST BOOKS
A division of Sterling Publishing Co., Inc.

New York / London
www.sterlingpublishing.com

Library of Congress Cataloging-in-Publication Data Available

10 9 8 7 6 5 4 3 2

Published by Hearst Books
A Division of Sterling Publishing Co., Inc.
387 Park Avenue South, New York, NY 10016

CosmoGIRL! and Hearst Books are trademarks of Hearst Communications, Inc.

www.cosmogirl.com

For information about custom editions, special sales, premium and corporate purchases, please
contact Sterling Special Sales Department at 800-805-5489 or specialsales@sterlingpublishing.com.

Distributed in Canada by Sterling Publishing
c/o Canadian Manda Group, 165 Dufferin Street
Toronto, Ontario, Canada M6K 3H6

Distributed in Australia by Capricorn Link (Australia) Pty. Ltd.
P.O. Box 704, Windsor, NSW 2756 Australia

Manufactured in China

Sterling ISBN 13: 978-1-58816-663-0

Photo credits: Chayo: p. 24; Alban Christ: pg. 91 (main); Aimee Herring: pg. 89, 90; Ellen Jong:
pg.7, 74, 91, 92, 99, 100, 101, 114, 115, 116; Stephen Lee: pg. 6, 56; Jennifer Livingston: pg. 104, 105,
106, 107; Eri Morita: pg. 61, 62, 63, 64, 65, 93, 94, 118, 119; Nino Muñoz: pg. 46, 71; Brooke Nipar:
pg. 5, 41, 42, 43, 44, 45, 85; Pascal Preti: pg. 10, 11, 12, 13, 14, 15, 16, 17, 52, 54, 55; Saye: pg. 7, 9,
47, 48, 72, 73, 95, 96, 97, 98, 102; Todd Selby: pg. 117; Michael E. Senior: pg. 6, 18, 19, 20, 21, 22, 25,
26, 27, 28, 29, 30, 31, 32, 33, 34, 35, 36, 37, 38, 39, 40, 49, 50, 51, 66, 67, 68, 69, 70, 76, 77, 78, 79, 80,
81, 82, 86, 87, 88; Hugo Tillman: pg. 58, 59, 60, 83, 84, 108, 109, 110, 111, 112, 113.

table of contents

chapter 1: the mind-body connection   23

chapter 2: cardio workouts   57

chapter 3: toning moves for every area 75

chapter 4: workouts for all occassions 103

susan's note
a letter from our editor-in-chief

Hey CosmoGIRL!s,

Welcome to our very first fitness book! I have to tell you something...you know what really impresses me about you? It's the fact that you're really into taking good care of yourselves. You know that a healthy body is essential for you to be able to do all the cool stuff you do in your life—whether it's performing in a play, being on the field hockey team, doing community service to give back, whatever. You're totally aware that when you're in good shape, you have tons of energy and can do so much! Being fit involves eating well, of course, but it also means getting good exercise. Every month in *CosmoGIRL!*, we give you a brand-new workout to try, all of them designed by top trainers. I love it when you write in to tell me you've tried the routine and that it's working! There's nothing like seeing results to keep you motivated, right? Well, here in this book are all sorts of workouts to help you tone your muscles and get you moving to keep your heart pumping, and best of all, all of them are FUN. Because that can be worst thing about exercise—when it gets so mundane that you'll come up with any excuse not to do it! So use this book on your own or with your friends. And let me know what you think of the moves—which ones are your favorites, which ones give you the quickest results, which ones had you walking funny the next day but worked so well that you decided to keep doing them—I love hearing what you have to say, so bring it on! Write to me at **susan@cosmogirl.com**. Now get moving, CG!s!

Love,

Susan

quiz
what's your
workout **style?**

Know how your favorite jeans fit so well you
feel like wearing them all the time? Well, your
workout should be like that—so *right* you want
to do it every day. Just answer these questions
to find your perfect fitness fit. You'll also find
other workout routines to try when you feel like
switching things up!

1. When working out, you like to sweat:
a. Not much at all.
• b. Just enough to know you're working hard.
c. A lot.

2. When you feel stressed, you:
a. Meditate or take long, deep breaths.
• b. Have fun with friends and try to forget about it.
c. Scream to release the tension.

3. What is your favorite part of working out?
a. Stretching: You find peace in feeling your tight muscles loosed up as you inhale and exhale.
• b. Cardio: you like to feel your heart pump and know you're burning major calories.
c. Taking a class or doing a video: You feed off the energy of the music and the motivation of the instructor.

4. When you are in school, you:
a. Have no problem paying attention to the subject matter and sitting in your seat for the full 50 minutes.
b. Might get bored, but you power through it, taking notes because you know the work is important.
c. Need group activities or hands-on assignments to keep your interest.

5. If you were a beverage from Starbucks, you would be a:
a. Chai tea.
b. Skim latte.
c. Java Chip Frappuccino.

scoring
Tally your answers, then find the right routine for you!

mostly a's: pilates
You want to feel like you're toning your body and working your mind, but you don't want the huffing and puffing associated with most traditional workouts. Pilates is perfect for you because it's an effective but low-impact way to build long, lean muscles. See pages 12-13 for moves.

mostly b's: cardio-toning circuit
To you, exercise is a necessity, not a favorite pastime. That's why you tend to stick to a set routine, so you can do it and get on with your life. You'll love our efficient combo of cardio and toning, since you can get both done at the same time. Turn to page 14-15 for moves.

mostly c's: sports drills
Energy's your middle name. And because you get bored with the same ol' routine, you prefer exercises that make you think fast and sweat. Your perfect workout is intense, with constant transitions from move to move, so you don't even have a chance to feel bored. See page 16-17 to get your moves.

pilates

Do these moves three times a week. All you'll need is a yoga mat or another kind of padding, like a towel. These pilates exercises will work your "core" muscles (the lower back and abs). Since every muscle in your body stems from your core, these moves will lengthen and tone your whole body. (They'll even make you appear taller!)

move 1: warm-up breathing exercise

a. Lie faceup and lift your legs toward the ceiling, with toes pointed. Make sure your entire spine is on the mat; there shouldn't be any space your fingers could slide under. Lift your arms and head (chin to chest) off the floor.

b. Keeping the rest of your body still, pump your arms up and down quickly, inhaling for five counts and exhaling for five. *Try 5 sets of 10 pumps, working up to 10 sets of 10.*

move 2: roll-ups

a. Lie faceup with knees bent, feet on the floor. Lift your head up, tucking your chin toward your chest. Hold onto the sides of your thighs. Press your spine into the mat.

b. Slowly roll up one vertebra at a time so you feel each part of your spine press into the mat. Keeping your chin tucked, release down again, one vertebra at a time. You should really feel this in your abs. *Repeat five times—slowly.*

move 3: leg circles

a. Lie faceup, lifting left leg to the ceiling while keeping right leg on the mat (bend leg if it's more comfortable). Point toes. With arms at sides, press spine into the mat.

b. Slowly circle left leg clockwise, keeping the rest of your body still. If that circle feels easy, make a larger one, but never let your leg touch the floor. *Do five circles in this direction and five counterclockwise. Repeat with right leg.*

move 4: single leg stretches

a. Lie faceup and pull your right knee to your chest. Place your right hand on that shin and left hand on your knee. Lift your leg about one to two feet off the floor and point your toes. Lift your head (chin to chest), spine flat on the mat.

b. Immediately switch legs. Alternate legs quickly 20 times. If this is too hard, point your straight leg toward the ceiling (it will take some weight off your abs).

move 5: spine stretches

a. Sit with your legs spread about 2 shoulder-widths apart. Flex your feet and stretch your arms out in front of you.

b. Tuck your chin to your chest and curl over toward your belly. Don't crunch over—you should slowly curl forward, stretching and lengthening your spine, as far as you can without collapsing forward. Your ultimate goal is to touch the top of your head to the mat. *Hold for one count, then roll back up. Repeat five times.*

cardio-toning **circuit**

These five moves are considered one circuit. Do two circuits (it'll take about 30 minutes to complete them both) three or four times a week. You'll need a pair of 3- to 10-pound dumbbells (start with 3 pounds and work up to 10). You'll work your heart, biceps, shoulders, arms, chest, back, legs, obliques, and abs.

move 1: crossover lunges with rows

a. Stand with feel shoulder-width apart. Hold arms perpendicular to your chest with palms up. Contract your abs.
b. Inhale and step back so your right foot crosses behind your left as you bend your knees. At the same time, squeeze shoulder blades together, pulling dumbbells back so your elbows point behind you. Exhale and return to starting position. Repeat on left side. *Do 15 lunges on each side.*

move 2: power squats

a. Stand with your hands on your hips and feet turned out a bit wider than shoulder-width apart. Bend your knees and squat down; your butt should stick out slightly. Make sure you keep your knees directly above your heels—they shouldn't go beyond your toes.
b. Explode into a big jump up, clicking your heels together. *Do 15 of these squat jumps in quick succession.*

move 3: standing crunches

a. Stand with feet shoulder-width apart, arms bent in front of you with hands in fists and palms facing you (like a boxer's guarding stance). Lift your left knee up as you twist your upper body and press your elbows down to meet it.
b. Repeat, lifting your right knee up this time and twisting to the right. *Alternate sides and continue this move until you feel your abs burn—at least 15 crunches on each side.*

move 4: pile squats with flies

a. Stand with knees slightly bent and feet shoulder-width apart; feet should be slightly turned out. Holding weights, reach your arms out to your sides with palms forward.

b. Bend your knees and do a squat—your butt should stick out a bit. Keep body weight on your heels, not your toes. As you squat, bring your arms together and turn your palms up. Make sure knees are directly above heels. *Do 15 reps.*

move 5: reverse lunges with arm raises

a. Holding weights at your sides, stand with feet shoulder-width apart, body weight on your heels, abs tight. Inhale and step back with left foot into a lunch (knee shouldn't touch the floor). As you lower yourself, lift arms in front of you, keeping palms down.

b. Exhale, stand up, then step back with the right foot and lunge. This time, extend your arms out to your sides. *Alternate legs and arm position until you've done 10 on each side.*

sports **drills**

Do three rounds of this series of moves three times a week. For the first round, do each move for 2 minutes. For the second, do each for 1 minute; for the third, 30 seconds. You'll need a basketball, two markers (like water bottles), a jump rope, and a stopwatch. You'll work your thighs, hamstrings, butt, shoulders, chest, biceps, abs, and lower back.

move 1: abductor step-outs

a. Set the markers in front of you, about 3–4 feet apart. Holding the ball, stand behind the left marker. Bend your knees and cross your right leg behind your left. Reach with the ball to your left and tap the floor with it.
b. Jump to the right marker, reaching up to the ceiling on the way. Land behind marker on the right. *Repeat crossover with your right leg. Do these from side to side until time is up.*

move 2: jump rope

Jump rope for the allotted time for that round.

move 3: squats

a. Stand with the ball in hand, then bend your knees and squat like you're sitting in an invisible chair. Don't let your knees extend past your toes. Tap the floor with the ball, keeping your back flat and your head up, looking forward.
b. Slowly return to standing while bringing the ball up all the way until it touches your chest (like you're doing biceps curls). *Repeat as many times as you can until time is up.*

move 4: step-out reaches

a. Hold the ball at your chest with elbows out. Now step out to the right and bend your right leg so your knee is directly over your ankle. Your left leg should be straight.

b. Pivot to the right, bending both legs into a lunge position. Reach your arms straight out in front of your body. Pivot back to the starting position, then repeat the step-out and lunch on the left side. *Do these until your time is up.*

move 5: long crunches

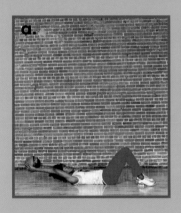
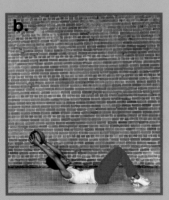

a. Holding the ball, lie on the ground with knees bent and feet on the floor. Reach your arms overhead (your biceps should brush your ears). Tuck in your chin to relax your neck.

b. Exhale and sit up, lifting your shoulder blades 4–6 inches off the floor without moving your arms. Keep your biceps glued to your ears. Your stomach muscles will really burn. *Exhaling as you lift up, repeat the crunch until your time is up.*

flex appeal

Stretching is one of those things you forget to do regularly, but when you do, it feels so good you wonder why you don't do it more often! Fitness expert Michelle LeMay, who created this workout, says stretching also helps prevent injuries by making your muscles more elastic and lubricating your joints. Do this 10-minute workout three times a week, holding each stretch for 10 seconds at a point where you feel muscles working but you're not in pain. In a month you'll be almost as loose as Elastigirl!

triceps stretch

stretches: triceps
Grasp your elbow as shown and pull it back (not toward your head). *Repeat on other side.*

caterpillar roll

stretches: neck, back, hamstrings, calves

a. With your hands on your thighs, stand with your knees bent slightly. Extend your left leg and place your heel on the ground (you'll feel the back of your left leg stretching).
b. Bend from your hips with a flat back, bringing your nose as close to your knee as you can.
c. Once you're at your maximum stretch, drop your head, then roll up, bringing your head up last. *Repeat with right leg extended.*

a.   b.   c.

lunge

stretches: legs, hips, shoulders, waist

a. Get into a lunge with your right knee above your right heel, left leg extended behind you. Drop your pelvis toward the floor to stretch the front of your hips.

b. Keeping your left hand on the floor, twist your torso to extend your right arm toward the ceiling. *Switch sides and repeat.*

bird of paradise

stretches: legs, hips, shoulders, lower back, waist

a. Sit with left leg extended to the side, right leg bent in. Extend your arms and breathe in.

b. Exhale as you reach your left arm over your ear toward your extended leg.

c. Inhale as you move back through position a, and then exhale as you extend your right arm. *Repeat with right leg extended.*

hip opener

stretches: hips, quads

a. Lie on your left hip, knees bent, resting your left forearm on the floor. Grasp your right ankle with your right hand and lift your right leg up slightly to separate your knees.

b. Use your right hand to guide your right foot behind you, parallel to the floor, until you feel the front of your hip stretch. *Repeat on your other side.*

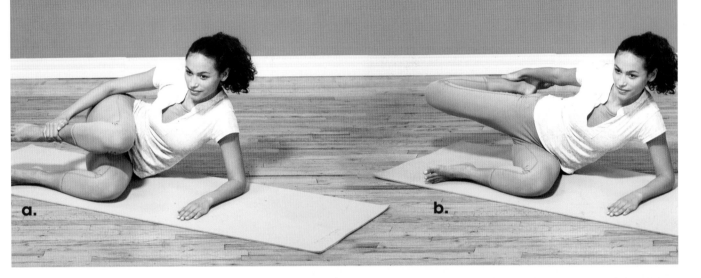

hip release

stretches: lower back, hips, butt

a. Lie on your back and cross your left ankle over your right thigh. Grasp below your right knee and pull gently (you'll feel a stretch on the outside of your left hip).

b. Hold knee as you rock lower torso to the right.
c. Roll back through position a, then rock lower torso to the left side. *Repeat the move on your other leg.*

the mind-body connection

body & soul **challenge**

It's time makeovers got a makeover. This program isn't just about looking better—it'll change the way you think about exercise and your life! Follow along for 4 months and you'll see great results!

basic **training**

The first step to transforming yourself? Learn this easy workout for a healthier body.

Trainer Jillian Michaels designed the first month's moves to help you learn proper form and build strength and cardio endurance. To get started, you need a set of 3- or 5-pound dumbbells or two full 20-ounce water bottles. Do each circuit three times before moving on to the next (it only takes 35 minutes total). In one month, you'll raise your fitness level so you can handle the upcoming challenges—plus you'll look *amazing*!

warm-up (5 minutes)

- Stretch out your arms, legs, and core muscles (try a sun salutation series; for how-to, go to **cosmogirl.com/bodysoul**).

circuit 1 (do 3 times)

- 10 push-ups (for how-to, go to **cosmogirl.com/bodysoul**)
- 30 seconds of mountain climbers
- 30 seconds of wall sit–arm raises

circuit 2 (do 3 times)

- 10 dumbbell rows (how-to at **cosmogirl.com/bodysoul**)
- 20 biceps curl lunges
- 20 single-leg pelvic thrusts (10 on each leg)

circuit 3 (do 3 times)

- 20 swing kicks
- 10 Superman toe crunches
- 3 minutes of shadowboxing (how-to at **cosmogirl.com/bodysoul**)

mountain climber

works: abs, shoulders, triceps, chest
a. Get in the position shown by placing your hands on the floor and pulling your right knee forward so your right foot is lined up with your butt.

b. Quickly bring your left knee in as you simultaneously jump back on your right leg, landing as shown. *Continue jumping your legs back and forth for 30 seconds.*

single-leg pelvic thrust

works: butt, thighs, lower back

a. Lie on your back with your arms at your sides, bending your left knee and extending your right leg toward the ceiling so the sole of your right foot is parallel to the ceiling.

b. Squeeze your butt muscles as you raise your hips toward the ceiling, keeping the sole of your right foot parallel to the ceiling. Slowly return to the starting position. *Do 10 reps, then switch legs and repeat.*

a.

b.

superman toe crunch

works: abs, back, butt, backs of legs

a. Lie facedown with arms and legs extended.
b. Simultaneously lift your arms and legs about six inches, hold for a second, then return to position a. *Do 5 reps, then flip over and get into position c.*

c. Lie faceup, legs extended, arms at your sides.
d. Raise your legs and reach hands toward your feet, "crunching" your abs. Hold for 10 seconds. *Return to position a and repeat series three times.*

a.

c.

b.

d.

soul goal

Feel like you're hitting an exercise wall? Try saying this mantra when the workout gets tough: "I am stronger than...." (Just fill in the blank.) For example, "I am stronger than this push-up." Or, "I am stronger than these swing kicks!" It really is just mind over matter!

swing kick

works: thighs, abs

Stand behind a chair that's mid-thigh high. Swing your left leg up and over the chair, tap your foot on the floor to the right of chair, then reverse your leg back over chair. *Do 10 reps, switch legs, repeat.*

wall sit–arm raise

works: thighs, shoulders

a. Holding dumbbells, "sit" against a wall.
b. With elbows slightly bent, raise your arms to shoulder level, then lower. *Holding the wall-sit, slowly raise and lower your arms for 30 seconds.*

a. **b.**

biceps curl lunge

works: biceps, butt, thighs, backs of legs

a. Stand with your feet hip-width apart, holding dumbbells as shown. Take a large step forward with your right leg.
b. Bend your knees to lower your body toward the floor as you curl the dumbbells up to your chest. Stop when your knees form 90-degree angles and the dumbbells are a few inches in front of your chest. Slowly return to position a. *Do 10 reps, then switch legs and repeat.*

a. **b.**

tone your muscles!

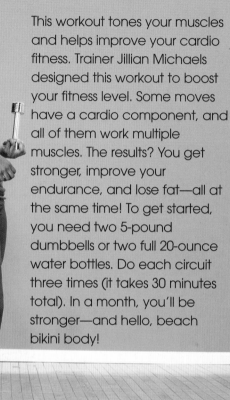

This workout tones your muscles and helps improve your cardio fitness. Trainer Jillian Michaels designed this workout to boost your fitness level. Some moves have a cardio component, and all of them work multiple muscles. The results? You get stronger, improve your endurance, and lose fat—all at the same time! To get started, you need two 5-pound dumbbells or two full 20-ounce water bottles. Do each circuit three times (it takes 30 minutes total). In a month, you'll be stronger—and hello, beach bikini body!

sumo squat with triceps extension

works: butt, thighs, calves, triceps

a. Hold a dumbbell above your head as shown and stand so your feet are wider than hip-width apart and your toes are pointed out.

b. Bend your knees to lower your butt 10 inches toward the floor (like you're sitting on a chair) while simultaneously bending your elbows to lower the dumbbell behind you. Straighten your arms and legs to return to position a. *Do 10 reps.*

a.   b.

circuit 1

- 30 seconds of plyos
- 20 lunges with torso twists (10 on each side)
- 30 seconds of squat thrusts (how-to: **cosmogirl.com/bodysoul**)

circuit 2

- 10 sumo squats with triceps extensions
- 1 minute of jumping jacks with biceps curls

circuit 3

- 10 back kicks with shoulder presses
- 1 set of pilates 100s
- 10 morning glories (how-to: **cosmogirl.com/bodysoul**)

pilates 100s

works: abs, lower back, legs

a. Lie on your back and raise your legs and feet so your body forms an L. Lift your arms a few inches off of the floor and stretch your hands past your butt, contracting your abs to lift your head and neck off of the floor.

b. Keeping your abs tight, pump your arms up (as shown in position b) and down (as in position a) 100 times.

back kick with shoulder press

works: shoulders, legs, butt, abs

a. With both hands, hold a dumbbell parallel to your chest, balancing on your right foot. Raise your left knee a bit higher than your hip.

b. Slowly bend forward, extending your left leg and arms parallel to the floor. Pull in your arms and leg as you return to position a. Repeat on the right. *Do 5 on each leg.*

lunge with torso twist

works: abs, lower back, thighs, butt

a. Stand with arms extended out to your sides, parallel to the floor.

b. Take a large step backward with your right foot. As you bend your knees to lower your butt toward the floor, twist your torso to the right and reach back to tap your right heel with your right hand. Push off your right foot and twist back to center to return to position a.

c. Repeat the lunge on the other side. *Do 20 lunges, alternating sides.*

challenge your soul!

Slow breathing helps you do moves requiring balance. Bonus: it helps you focus during tests too!

plyos

a. **b.** **c.**

works: butt, thighs, calves
a. With arms at your sides, place your right foot on a step 6 to 12 inches high.
b. Pushing off your right foot, explode upward and jump as high as you can.
c. Land with your left foot on the step and your right on the floor, then immediately jump again, this time landing in position a. Continue jumping (alternating feet) for 30 seconds.

jumping jacks with biceps curls

works: thighs, calves, abs, biceps
a. Stand with feet together, arms extended at your sides. Hold a dumbbell in each hand, palms up.

a.

b. Jump your feet out while bending your elbows to bring dumbbells near your ears. Jump in as you straighten arms. *Continue for 1 minute.*

b.

overcome a **plateau**

When the going gets tough, the tough... use this workout to overcome a fitness plateau!

A plateau or boredom can happen when your muscles get too used to the exercises you've been doing. So, trainer Jillian Michaels created a workout with new versions of the basic moves you already know (like a regular ol' push-up or squat). Just the act of learning these moves can help prevent boredom, and the fact that they engage new muscles can help you see positive changes in your body. To get started, you need two 5-pound dumbbells or two full 20-ounce water bottles. Do each circuit below 3 times before moving on to the next (it should take 30 minutes total). In a month, you'll be saying *hellooooo* tank-top and miniskirt season!

circuit 1
- 12 alternating victory lunges
- 12 Russian twists

circuit 2
- 20 king squats (10 on each leg)
- 10 walk-about push-ups

circuit 3
- 30 seconds standing mountain climbers
- 20 alternating plank twists (10 with each leg)
- 12 one-leg bench dips (how-tos: **cosmogirl.com/bodysoul**)

victory lunge

works: arms, butt, thighs, legs
a. Holding a water bottle in each hand, stand straight with your arms extended above your head so the water bottles are shoulder-width apart (keep them in this position through the entire move).
b. Take one large step backwards with your left leg, then lower your left knee to the floor so both your legs form 90-degree angles.
c. Bring your right leg back to place your right knee next to your left so you're in a kneeling position.
d. Step your left leg forward and place your left foot on the floor so both knees form right angles, then push off your left foot to return to the starting position.
Repeat the entire move on your other side by first stepping back with your right foot. *Do 12 reps; each rep consists of moving through the positions twice (once starting with your left leg, once starting with your right leg).*

russian twist

a.

b.

works: abs, obliques

a. Lie on the floor with your knees bent as if you're about to do a sit-up. Extend your arms towards the ceiling, and place your palms together. Keeping your feet on the ground (you can tuck them under dumbbells or your couch to make it easier), use your abs to lift your torso off the floor until your arms are parallel to your thighs (as shown).

b. Keeping your abs engaged, twist your torso to the left as far as you comfortably can (as shown), back to center, then to the right as far as you comfortably can, then back to center. Finish by rolling down until your back is resting on the floor. *Do 12 reps.*

king squat

works: thighs, butt, legs

a. With your hands on your hips, stand two feet in front of a chair, then reach your right leg behind you and rest the laces of your sneaker on the center of the chair.

b. Bend your left knee until your left thigh is almost parallel to the floor, then straighten your left leg to return to position a. *Do 20 reps, then switch legs and repeat.*

a.

b.

standing mountain climber

works: shoulders, butt, legs

a. Get into position a of the alternating victory lunge, then bring your left hand down to shoulder level and bring your left knee up as high as you can.

a.

b. Begin "climbing" by simultaneously extending your left arm and lifting your right knee as you bring down your right hand and lower your left knee. *Continue climbing by alternating between position a and b in smooth, controlled movements. "Climb" for 30 seconds.*

b.

walkabout push-up

works: abs, arms

a. Keeping your legs straight (with soft knees), bend over and place your hands on the floor as close to your toes as possible. (The more flexible you are, the closer your hands will be to your toes).

a.

b. Slowly walk your hands out about four feet.

b.

c. Drop your butt and engage your abs to get into a plank position with your hands beneath your shoulders.

c.

d. Do one regular push-up, then walk your hands back towards your feet, and finish the rep by slowly standing up. *Do 10 reps.*

d.

works: abs, arms, obliques

a. Get into a plank position with your abs tight and your hands placed directly beneath your shoulders.

b. Keeping your abs engaged, rotate your entire torso by bringing your left knee in as far as you can towards your right armpit. Twist back to center as you extend your leg return to position a. Repeat the move on your other side by bringing your right knee in towards your left armpit. *Do 20 reps (10 on each side).*

challenge your soul!

Switching your location each time you work out (whether going outside or just to a different room) can engage your brain and make workouts more stimulating.

love your workout!

These new moves are so much fun you'll want to do 'em all the time!

Trainer Jillian Michaels designed this workout to take you away from routine moves. Do the workout from beginning to end two times in a row (it takes about 25 minutes). Some of the moves might feel goofy the first time you try them, but that's the point! Doing them helps you lose your inhibitions so you can think of exercise like you did when you were a kid. You know, when going out to play wasn't "exercise"—it was just *fun!*

s.a.q. (speed, agility, quickness) drill

a.   b.   c.   d.

works: obliques, butt, thighs, calves

a. With your elbows bent so your hands are waist-level, stand with your feet together, knees soft.

b. Jump and twist the lower half of your body to the left, landing with your toes pointed left.

c. Jump and twist back to center, landing with your toes forward.

d. Jump and twist your lower half to the right, landing with toes pointed right. *Jump "left-center-right-center" as fast as you can for 1 minute.*

corkscrew

works: abs, obliques

a. Lie on your back, extend your arms behind your head, and grasp the legs of a chair to stabilize yourself. Keeping your abs tight, raise your legs so your body forms an L shape.

b. Use your abs to lift your butt off the floor as you twist your legs to the left as far as you can, then slowly lower your butt to the floor as you twist your legs back to center.

c. Repeat the move on your other side. *Do 3 sets of 12 corkscrews.*

burpies

works: arms, abs, thighs, calves

a. With your feet about shoulder-width apart, squat down and place your palms on the floor about 6 inches in front of your toes.

b. Push off the balls of your feet to kick your legs out behind you, landing in a push-up position with your hands beneath your shoulders.

c. Return to position a by jumping your feet back in toward your hands.

d. From the squat position, explode upward to jump as high as you can, then land back in a squatting position and immediately begin the next burpie. *Do 3 sets of 12 burpies.*

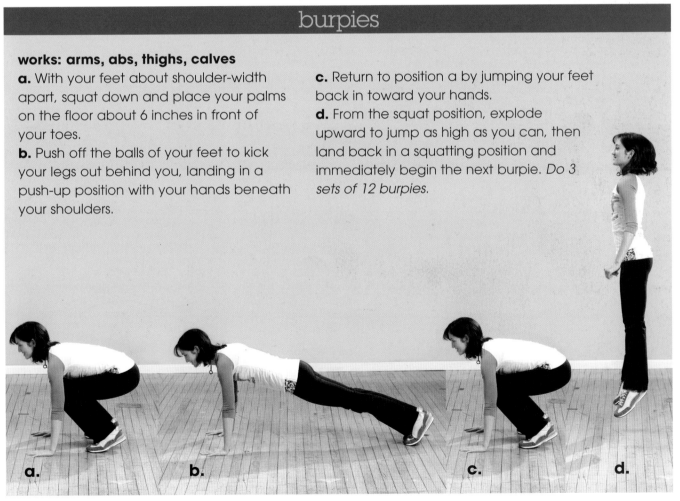

a.   b.   c.   d.

donkey kick

works: arms, abs, butt, legs

a. Bend over and place your palms on the floor three feet in front of your toes.
b. Extend your left leg as high as you can behind you.
c. Bend your right knee slightly, then push off your right foot as if you were trying to

kick into a handstand. Let your body swing up, then back toward the floor.
d. Land on your right foot. *Do 12 kicks, then switch sides and do 12 more.*

a.   b.   c.   d.

rock star jump

works: butt, legs

a. Stand with your feet about shoulder-width apart, then jump straight up as high as you can and try to touch your heels to your butt.
b. Land with your knees soft, then immediately jump up again. *Do 3 sets of 12 jumps.*

a.   b.

challenge your soul!

Trouble getting motivated to work out? Think of it this way: You'll be finished in less time than it takes to watch an episode of your favorite TV show (and then you can actually watch your favorite TV show!).

yoga—with a **twist**

Grab a friend and tie the knot! Well, sorta. These partner yoga poses stretch and strengthen your arms, abs, back, and legs.

You know exercise is good for your body and mind, but sometimes it's just the last thing you want to do. That's why working out with a friend is such a smart idea—it makes exercising more fun and it's hard to skip it when there's someone else counting on you! This workout, created with Bess Gallanis, author of *Yoga Chick, A Hip Guide to Everything Om,* features partner poses that improve your flexibility and balance and tone your muscles. Do the workout everyday (it only takes about 10 to 15 minutes) or whenever you want to spend time

with a friend. You may look weird all tied up in knots—but who cares? It's about how you *feel*! And just imagine how you'll kick butt the next time you play Twister!

seated forward bend

stretches: lower back and legs.
Sit on the floor with legs extended and toes touching. Now reach to the ceiling to lengthen your spine, then reach your arms toward your partner until your fingertips touch. If one (of both) of you can't reach all the way, it's okay to bend your knees. As along as you feel a stretch in your back and hamstrings, the pose is working. *Hold for three to five slow, deep breaths.*

partners child's pose

bottom position stretches lower back. Top position stretches upper and lower back.
One partner gets into child's pose: Sit with your knees bent so your butt rests on your heels, then lower your forehead to the floor and extend your arms, palms down. The other partner lays back-to-back on top so her butt rests just below her partner's waist, her heels rest on the floor, and her arms and legs are fully extended as shown. *Hold for three to five slow, breaths; switch positions and repeat.*

partners twist

stretches: back, shoulders, and spine; tones: your arms and abs.

a. Sit cross-legged, back-to-back with your partner. Extend your arms out to your sides, parallel to the floor, and clasp hands. Inhale and exhale together until your breathing is synchronized, then, keeping your abs tight, slowly twist your torsos to the right and hold for three slow, deep breaths.

a.

b. Slowly twist your torsos to the left and hold for three deep breaths. *Repeat the sequence three times.*

b.

warrior 2 pose for 2

stretches: back and legs; tones: legs, abs, and arms; improves balance.

Stand one partner behind the other, then take a large step with your right foot and turn it out so it's perpendicular to your left foot. Bend your right knee until your thigh is almost parallel to the floor. Extend your arms parallel to the floor, palms down.

Next, the front partner balances her arms on the rear partner's arms. Hold for three to five slow, deep breaths; switch positions and repeat. *Then, repeat sequence on your left side (bending your left knee).*

child's pose/downward dog

child's pose stretches lower back. Downward dog stretches hamstrings; tones back, arms and, legs.

One partner should get into child's pose (see partners child's pose for directions), grasping the ankles of the other partner, who stands facing her. The standing partner then gets into downward dog by reaching over her partner and placing her hands palms-in on either side of her partner's hips so her body forms an upside-down V, with her arms extended and legs straight (or almost straight). *Hold for three to five slow, deep breaths; switch positions and repeat.*

power yoga

Too cold to go for a run? No worries! You can still get a sexy body with *CG!*'s power yoga workout by Beryl Bender Birch. Just clear a space in your house and do this routine four to five times a week for 30 minutes. You'll look hot and feel more fit, focused, and confident—bonus!

sun salutation

These poses will strengthen your body and get your heart pumping since they're done in a "flow." (You'll string them together so you're moving from one right into the next.) Start off slowly until you're familiar with each pose, then build to a faster pace. Breathe slowly through your nose, inhaling and exhaling in a relaxed rhythm. Start with 2–3 reps (all 17 poses together equal one rep), then add 2–3 more every 3 weeks until you can do 10–15 reps. Remember: Don't force yourself into the poses. If it hurts, ease up!

1. With your feet touching, inhale, bend your knees, and raise your arms over your head. Put your palms together, and look at your thumbs. Drop your shoulders (so they aren't near your ears).

2. Exhale as you straighten your legs, and bend forward toward your toes, reaching your fingers to the floor. If you need to, bend your knees slightly so you can reach the ground.

3. With your fingertips on the floor, inhale and gently look up. Push your butt to the ceiling and drop your shoulders.

4. Exhale and lower yourself into a pre-push-up position (it should look like the bottom point of a push-up) so that all of your weight is on your palms and your toes. Look out in front of you. This is known as the Four-Limbed Stick Pose.

5. Inhale as you straighten your arms, and slide your hips forward. Gently look up, and drop your shoulders—they shouldn't be near your ears. Your toes should be pointed with your legs on the floor. This is known as Face Up Dog.

6. Exhale and turn your toes under (so you're on the balls of your feet). Push into an upside-down V, feet parallel to each other. Hands should be shoulder-width apart and fingers spread so your weight is evenly distributed. You should feel like your hips are being pulled up to the ceiling. This is known as Face Down Dog.

7. Now inhale and step your right foot up between your hands, then bend your knee so it's over your ankle. Turn your left heel inward—your arch will be perpendicular to your right heel. Lift up your arms, palms together, then look up. This is known as Warrior 1.

Finish by repeating the poses you now know.

8.	Exhale, repeat 4.
9.	Inhale, repeat 5.
10.	Exhale, repeat 6.
11.	Inhale, repeat 7 but now on the left.
12.	Exhale, repeat 4.
13.	Inhale, repeat 5.
14.	Exhale, repeat 6.
15.	Inhale, repeat 3.
16.	Exhale, repeat 2.
17.	Inhale, repeat 1.

Once you're comfortable doing the salutation without looking at the book, try these poses after your last salutation (you started with 2–3 and will work up to 10–15). Unlike the salutation poses, you won't repeat these. Instead, hold each for 5 slow breaths (breathing in then out = one). Do the poses 4–5 times a week. They'll tone your bod and make your lower back and hips more flexible.

extended triangle pose

1a. Inhale and jump so your legs are 3 feet apart. Turn your right foot out—your heel will be perpendicular to the arch of your left foot. Extend your arms out to shoulder level, then bend to the right as you gently look up to your left hand.

1b. Bend until your hand reaches your ankle (or shin, if that feels more comfortable). You'll feel a nice stretch in your right hamstring. Your arms, shoulders, and hips should be in a straight line with your left arm reaching up. Look up at your thumb, and hold for 5 breaths. *Repeat on your left side.*

extended side angle pose

2a. Inhale and, while standing, extend your legs 4 feet apart. Point your right foot to the right. Your left toes should face forward. Lift your arms out to your sides.

2b. Exhale and, in a fluid motion, bend your right knee so it's directly over your ankle. Place your right palm on the floor by the inside of your foot, and let your left arm extend up. Keep your shoulders in a straight line, and look up at your thumb. *Hold for 5 breaths, then repeat 2a and 2b on your left side.*

big toe pose

3a. Stand with your feet parallel and 6 inches apart. Inhale and grab your big toes with your first 2 fingers. If you need to, bend your knees to reach your toes. Look up gently, and push your butt toward the ceiling.

3b. Now exhale and fold deeper at the hips. Use your arms and shoulders to pull your upper body toward your thighs. Look at your legs, and try not to round your back. *Hold for 5 breaths.*

surfer yoga

This yoga workout, designed for beginning surfers by Hawaii's Kelea Surf Spa, strengthens your upper body so that you'll look great on land—and in the barrel!

Have you ever met an out-of-shape surfer? Didn't think so! You too can get a rad surfer's body (bleach blond hair not necessarily included!) with this simple Vinyasa yoga workout. Many surfers do yoga to stay in shape because it strengthens and lengthens muscles in the arms, shoulders, legs, and back—all muscles that are used in surfing. But even if you don't surf, this workout will give you a strong, lean body. So, to begin...

- Do the yoga routine on the next page two days a week, working up to four days. You'll need a yoga mat and a set of 2- to 5-pound weights (these are optional).
- Do 20 minutes of freestyle swimming two days a week on your days off from yoga. Improve your stroke by adding three more laps each time you swim. This will really get your body conditioned for surfing.
- Do this regimen for a full month. You'll see results within two weeks, but put in a full month before you attempt to surf to be sure your body's strong enough to hit the waves. Cowabunga, CosmoGIRL!

Do these poses one right after another (it takes 20–30 minutes).
After move 12, lie on your back and rest for two minutes.

1. cow

works: back, spine, abs

Get down on all fours with knees aligned under hips and wrists under shoulders. Tops of toes should be on the mat and your fingers spread out. Inhale through your nose and push your chest forward and your butt bones up so your back is sloped. Immediately move to pose 2.

2. cat

works: back, spine, abs

Exhale through your nose and push your spine up to the sky so that your back rounds out and you look like a frightened cat. Drop your head and slowly relax your neck. In a fluid motion, repeat poses 1 and 2 (alternating back and forth) a total of five times.

3. cat bow (a)

works: arms, shoulders

From all fours, lean forward, keeping your knees on the ground and bending your elbows up against your ribs (like a push-up, but with your butt sticking up). Fingers should point forward, and chest should be 4–7 inches off the ground. Proceed immediately to pose 4.

4. cat bow (b)

works: arms, shoulders

Exhale and release your chest down so it's about 2 inches off the mat and your knees are still on it. You'll really feel this in your arms. Immediately inhale as you push yourself back up to pose 3, then repeat the push-up slowly (poses 3 and 4) three to five times.

5. down dog

works: arms, shoulders, legs

From pose 4, exhale and straighten your legs and arms so that your butt lifts straight up and your body forms an upside-down V. Keep hands shoulder-width apart, legs hip-width apart. Use arms to push your shoulder blades up toward the sky. Hold for three breaths.

6. plank

works: arms, shoulders, legs

From pose 5, exhale and lower your body so that it's in a flat push-up position. Your hands should be as wide as your chest, with your elbows beneath your shoulders. Look down at the mat. Your abs and butt should be flexed and tight. Inhale and move on to pose 7.

7. chaturanga

works: arms, shoulders, legs, butt, abs

Exhale, bending your arms and lowering yourself into a low push-up position. Inhale and immediately push back up to plank (pose 6). Repeat poses 5–7—down dog to plank to chaturanga to down dog—a total of three to five times.

8. locust

works: butt; lengthens: spine, abs

Lie on your stomach with arms at your sides, forehead on the mat. Inhale, lifting your chest and legs up and out, keeping your legs together. Look at the ground in front of you. Arms should be lifted, your butt and hamstrings tight. Hold the pose for three long breaths.

9. neck rotation

lengthens: neck

Exhale and lower your chest and legs to the ground. Turn your head to one side, resting your cheek on the mat with your arms at your sides, palms up. Rest for three long breaths. Repeat poses 8 and 9 three times total. Rest on the opposite cheek after each locust.

10. bow

works: chest, abs, back

From pose 9, bend your knees, reach back, and grab the top of your ankles. Use your leg muscles to push your ankles back into your hands—it'll help you lift your toes and chest up. If your hip bones dig into the ground, fold mat over for padding. Hold for three breaths.

11. forward bend

lengthens: back

Release pose 10 and lie facedown. Roll onto your back, bend your knees, and sit up. Stretch your legs out in front of you, and bend forward to grab your toes (bend your knees if you can't reach your toes). Keep your back as straight as possible. Hold for three breaths.

12. warrior 2

works: arms, legs

Holding weights, stand up and step back with your right foot. Turn it out so it's perpendicular to your left (left heel should be in line with right arch). Bend left leg so your knee's over your ankle. Stretch arms out. Hold for three breaths. Repeat with right foot forward.

take a **hike**

Have you heard of this place where you can work out without sweaty guys grunting on machines next to you? It's called the outdoors—and membership is free!

Hiking is already great cardio, but certified trainer Melanie Webb, owner of Sol Fitness Adventures in Washington, D.C., created these moves to turn a nature walk into a strengthening workout for your arms, abs, and legs too! Do these moves three times a week during a 45-minute hike and your arms and legs will look more defined in about six weeks. If you don't live near hiking trails, go for a brisk walk through a safe park path or a hilly section of your neighborhood. Happy trails!

sun salutation

stretches: legs and back

a. Stand with your feet slightly apart, then slowly inhale as you raise your chin and look toward the sky while extending your arms above your head, palms facing each other. *Hold for 5 counts.*

b. Slowly exhale as you bend from your hips; try to place your palms on the ground on either side of your feet. *Hold for 5 counts.*

boulder push-up

strengthens: arms and chest

a. Get into a push-up position so your hands are placed on a boulder (or the back of a bench) that's below chest level. With feet hip-width apart, balance on the balls of your feet.

b. Keeping your body in a straight line, inhale as you do a push-up by bending your elbows until your chest almost touches the rock. Exhale as you return to start. *Do 3 sets of 12 push-ups.*

tree sit

strengthens: legs, butt, abs
Stand with your back against a tree. With feet hip-width apart, slide into a sitting position until your knees are bent in a 90-degree angle. Keeping your abs pulled in tight, rest your hands on top of your thighs and hold for 1 minute. Rest and repeat twice.

boulder dip

strengthens: triceps
a. Sitting on a boulder or bench between knee and hip level, plant palms next to hips. With legs out, slide hips forward, off boulder.

b. Lower butt toward the ground by bending your elbows until they form right angles. Lift back up to position a. Do 3 sets of 12 dips.

born to **run**

If your idea of a marathon involves watching reruns of your favorite show, this plan will change that! You'll learn to love running and start to feel stronger in about two weeks!

get started

- When you're just beginning to run, don't push yourself too hard. You'll become a better runner that way and *want* to stick with it.
- Stay motivated by running with a friend.
- Instead of thinking about getting your run over with, focus on how your body moves and soak in the scenery. You'll have more fun!
- Don't get discouraged by thinking you should run faster or farther. Do only what feels right—that's how you become a runner for *life.*

your clothes

Wear stretchy fitted shirts, and shorts or pants that won't get in the way of body movement. Also, get a sports bra labeled "Dri-Fit"—it'll really absorb your sweat. Do jumping jacks in the dressing room to make sure it supports but isn't so tight under your pits or around your torso that it's uncomfortable.

your shoes

Shop at a specialty running store, where experts can help you avoid injury by telling you whether your arch is high or low, how flexible your feet are, and whether your feet roll in- or outward. Try on several pairs to find one of these three types that is the most comfortable.

stability

These give support and cushioning and are great starter shoes for beginners who aren't sure how their feet move.

cushion

They're less supportive but soft, so these are good for street runners, advanced runners, or those who have strong feet.

motion control

These support the sides of your feet, keeping them from rolling too far inward or outward (if that's a problem for you).

rule 1: make a plan
Run 3 times a week (no more than 4) for 30 minutes, including warm-up. Your muscles need rest to relax and get stronger, so take a day off between each run.

rule 2: warm up
Warm up by walking fast for 5 minutes before you run.

rule 3: try intervals
When you're first starting out, run for 3–5 minutes, then walk fast for 1-2, and repeat until you hit 30 minutes. If you're breathing hard, or if something hurts, slow down.

rule 4: fuel yourself
Eat foods that are rich in iron (chicken, soy products, dark leafy greens), potassium (potatoes, bananas, apples), and vitamin B12 (fortified cereals, meats, milk).

rule 5: know your body
If you feel faint while running, you're probably dehydrated. Be sure to drink at least 8 glasses of water during the day to keep hydrated. If you're fatigued after running for less than 15 minutes, get more iron and B12 in your diet.

get **toned**

For a fully toned and strong body, do these three strengthening exercises after running.

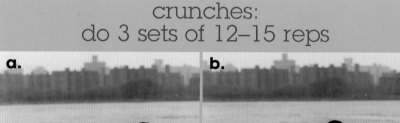

crunches: do 3 sets of 12–15 reps

a. Lie on your back, knees bent, with hands behind your head.
b. Exhale as you crunch toward your knees (until shoulder blades are off the floor), then inhale as you release.

lunges: do 3 sets of 12–15 reps on each side

a. Inhale and stand tall with your right foot two feet in front of you and your left leg extended back.
b. Exhale as you bend knees until your right leg is at 90 degrees (don't let your knee overextend). *Come up, then repeat on the right.*

a. Place your hands on the floor, slightly wider than shoulder distance, with knees resting on the ground and feet toward the sky.

b. Lower yourself toward the floor as you inhale and push yourself up as you exhale. *Repeat. Make sure you keep your spine straight as you do these—your butt shouldn't stick up.*

stretch **out**

End each workout by stretching to keep muscles injury-free. Hold each move for 30 seconds.

calves

Step forward on your right foot with your knee bent. Your left leg should be behind you with your left heel planted. Lean forward slightly until you feel a stretch in your left calf. *Hold, then switch sides.*

hamstrings

Stretch your right leg in front of your body, with your foot flexed and your heel on the floor. Bend your left knee. Lean toward your left thigh until you feel a stretch in your right hamstring. *Repeat on the left.*

quadriceps

Bend your left knee and lift your foot behind you toward your butt. Hold it in place with your left hand. Bend your right knee slightly and keep your knees in line with each other. *Hold, then switch legs.*

cardio workouts

dance, dance, **dance!**

Hey, dance machines: This choreographed workout is so much fun you won't realize it's also a killer cardio session. Now show us your moves!

We asked the pros from New York City's Broadway Dance Center to show us moves from four Broadway shows that can get your heart pumping and burn calories while toning your arms, legs, and abs. Just put on any rug-cutting song (either one from a show's cast recording or Usher!) and do the moves. Try them in the order here, or put together your own combo (like b+a+c+d). To get the hang of it, learn each move without music: When you put the positions shown together, you'll see they're one dance move. (You may even recognize it from the show!) Hold each position in the move for one count (a count is one beat of music). Then do a combination of all the moves to two songs every day, working up to four or five songs in a row. They may seem hard at first, but once they click you'll know them for life! Soon you'll have the energy of a dancer, plus a rockin' toned body!

charleston (move from **Chicago**)

a.   b.   c.

works: shoulders and quads
a. Hold your right arm straight up (palm facing forward) and your left arm at shoulder level. Kick your left leg in front of you about 1 foot off the ground. Put your weight on your right leg and keep it slightly bent.
b. In one fluid movement, swing your left leg back so it's 2 feet behind your right leg. Bend both arms so that your elbows are pointing out, with your shoulders in a straight line, and touch your fingertips together right in front of your chest.
c. Step back about 3 feet with your right leg and then lunge, making sure your knee doesn't go past your toes, and lean forward. Then turn your left knee and foot out. Point your right arm down and your left arm up. Go back to step b, then step a. Do two sets (steps a, b, c, b, a = one set). *Rest, then do two more.*

trench step (move from **42nd Street**)

a.

b.

works: quads, deltoids, and abs

a. Step your left foot 2 feet in front of your body, toes pointed slightly to the left. Bend your left leg, but don't extend your knee over your toes. Then lift your right foot 2 inches off the floor behind you so your weight is on your left leg. Extend your right arm so it's at a 45-degree angle above your right shoulder and drop your left arm 45 degrees (your hands should look like blades).
b. Jump to change positions, bringing your right foot in front and extending your left leg back behind you (your left arm should be forward). Hop back to step a. (Each jump takes one count.) *Do two sets of eight, rest for eight counts, then do two more.*

tiny twist (move from **Hairspray**)

a.

b.

c.

works: obliques and calves

a. Stand on the balls of your feet with your knees bent. Put arms up and slightly to the right, with hands in fists. With your upper body facing forward, twist your knees and hips to the left. Twist your arms in the opposite direction.
b. Hop on the balls of your feet once so your hips and knees switch sides and are now facing toward the right while your arms are twisting to the left—in opposite directions. As you're twisting your body, bring your arms down slightly lower than your shoulders.
c. Hop and twist back to the left, arms hanging down to the right. Go back to step b, then a. *Do four sets (steps a, b, c, b, a = one set), rest, then do four more sets.*

plié pull (move from **Bombay Dreams**)

a.

b.

c.

d.

e.

f.

works: quads, shoulders, and butt

a. Start with your legs hip-width apart, knees bent, and toes angled out (this position is called a plié). With your palms facing down, hold your right arm to the side at shoulder level, your left in front of you and slightly to the right. Bounce once on the balls of your feet.

b. Bounce again, but this time move your arms so they're straight in front of you at shoulder level (your arms should flow from step a to step b).

c. Instead of bouncing a third time, pull your left leg up to hip level so your foot is about 2 feet above the floor (your foot should be flexed and your knee bent). As you pull your leg up to the side, tighten your abs for balance and fold your arms in so your elbows are bent out to the side with fingertips almost touching. Hold for two counts.

d. Bring your left leg down and do step a again, putting your right arm in front this time. Bounce once.

e. Repeat step b.

f. Repeat step c, pulling up your right leg this time. Hold for two counts. Do four sets (steps a–f = one set). *Rest for eight counts, then do six more sets.*

hard-core
workout!

Who says punk's just for moshing? Crank up the music and do these heart-pumping, muscle-toning moves for a great body!

Certified aerobics instructors Maura Jasper and Hilken Mancini created punk rock aerobics to save themselves—and you—from all of the lame, boring workouts out there. To get started, grab two 3–5 -pound objects you can comfortably use as weights (try two 1-liter bottles filled with water). Then warm up with 10 minutes of dancing or running in place to your favorite punk CD. Do this workout three to five days a week for a strong—and vicious—body.

a.

b.

works: your heart

a. Stand with feet a little wider than hip-distance apart with left foot turned out to a 45-degree angle and left knee slightly bent. Keep your right leg straight. Bring your left arm straight out to your side with your hand in a fist.

b. The next two steps should be done in a fluid motion. Swing your right arm forward in a circular motion; it should meet your left arm and continue around to make a circle. As you do this with your arms, kick your right leg across your left (on an angle) so it's even with your left arm.
Bend and lift your right knee until your heel lines up with your left knee and jump up and down on your left leg. Keep swinging your arm in a circle (like you're a rock star shredding a guitar!). Repeat on the right (right leg bent, right arm out to the side). *Do this for one minute on each side to the music's beat.*

iron man

a.

b.

works: arms, chest, back

a. Hold one weight vertically in each hand so palms face forward; stand with feet shoulder-width apart and knees slightly bent. Bring arms out to your sides and bend them into a solid L shape (like you're showing off your insane bicep muscles!).

b. Hold your abs in tight as you move your arms toward each other, in front of your face. Your forearms should be parallel. Don't drop your arms between steps a and b. Try 10 reps of b. *Do six sets, resting arms at your sides for a few seconds between each set.*

fire hydrants

works: butt and thighs

a. Get down on all fours with your head up and your focus forward. Keeping your left knee bent (see photo), lift your left leg out to the side in a 90-degree angle (or as high as you can).

b. Now extend and straighten your left leg so your toes are pointed and straight out to the side. Then bend your knee again and return to starting position. Repeat slowly 10–12 times on each leg. *Try three sets of these kicks. For the best workout, your butt and thigh muscles should be burning (yup!) at the end of each set.*

gut buster

works: abs

a. Lie on your back with your arms at your sides, palms facing down. Lift your legs, with knees bent in a 90-degree angle. Your focus should be on the ceiling.

b. Keeping your lower back pressed to the floor, slowly straighten your left leg and lower it so that it almost touches the floor. Don't use your arms to make it easier. Hold for one count and return to starting position. Repeat on the right leg immediately. *Try three sets of 20 switches, alternating fluidly from right to left.*

moving unit

works: butt and hamstrings

a. Lie on your back with knees bent and arms resting at your sides, palms down. Straighten your right leg up toward the ceiling so it's in line with your left knee.

b. Press your shoulders and upper back into the floor as you squeeze your butt and lift your hips off the floor; hold. Keep leg extended and abs tight throughout the move. Don't use your arms to help lift your body weight—just your leg and butt muscles. Slowly release your butt back down to the floor. Do 10 of these lifts. Repeat with left leg lifted, right foot on the floor. *Try three sets of 10 on each side, resting in between.*

body by **bollywood**

Get ready to shake your booty with the sexy dance that doubles as a full-body cardio workout!

Bhangra (a Punjabi word) is a traditional Indian folk celebration dance that's fun and an awesome toning workout. These moves come from Sarina Jain, creator of The Masala Bhangra Workout. Do them three times a week—you need a scarf or cloth napkin to dance with and bhangra music. No shoes required!

bollywood bhangra

a.   b.   c.

works: legs, hips, abs

a. Start with your legs together so that your knees and ankles are touching. Bend your knees slightly. Place your left hand on your hip and your right hand on your head above your ear with your elbow pointing out to the side.

b. Look to your left and do four bunnylike hops in that direction. Squeeze your abs tight to give you the energy to hop and swing your hip to the left in sync with the hop. Make sure your knees are glued together the entire time.

c. Switch your arms (right hand on your hip and left hand on your head above your ear). Look to the right and repeat the four hops and hip moves in that direction. *Do a total to four sets of steps b and c to the beat of the music.*

bhangra push

a.   b.

works: shoulders, legs

a. Put your left hand on your hip and raise your right arm toward the ceiling. Take a step forward with your right foot, then push off the ball of that foot (pushing down on your toes and then lifting up).

b. Continue to lift your right foot four times as you move clockwise in a semicircle. Shrug your shoulders to the beat as you dance, but keep your left hand on your hip and your right arm raised. Do four semicircles to the right.

c. (Not shown) Switch to your right hand and left foot and repeat the semicircle counterclockwise. Do this for four counts, repeating steps 1 and 2. *Repeat steps 1–3 three more times.*

dhol beat

a.

b.

c.

d.

works: arms, shoulders, legs

a. Stand with your feet shoulder-width apart, arms at your sides. This is your starting position. Then step forward with your right foot, about 12 inches in front of you, and lean your upper body in the same direction. Now act like you're banging on an imaginary drum (banging your right hand down first).

b. As you stomp, bang your right hand down in unison for three counts (count: "And one, and two, and three").

c. Return to the starting position. Step your right foot back behind your body (about 12 inches) and lean backward slightly. Lift your right arm up and your left arm to the side and bend them slightly for balance. Keep your hands relaxed.

d. Shrug your shoulders for three counts (push harder on the "down" part of the shrug). Then add a toe tap: Lift your left leg, point your toes, and tap your foot on the floor three times—the shrug and toe tap should be done in unison. *Repeat all four moves four times. Move through steps a–2b in a continuous series, without pausing or resting.*

basic bhangra

a.

b.

works: deltoids, shoulders, biceps

a. Begin by stepping your right heel out in front of your body, bringing it back to the starting position, then stepping your left heel out. Continue this alternating heel-touch-step to the beat of the music.

b. Keep your feet moving as you lift your arms up so your hands reach toward the ceiling. Bend your elbows so that your arms form a U shape. Shrug your shoulders, putting more emphasis on the "down" part of the shrug. At the same time, twist your hands like you're unscrewing two light bulbs that are above you. You should be doing the heel-touch-step with your arms lifted, shoulders shrugging and hands twisting—all at the same time. *Do this for eight counts (count "And one, and two, and three," and so on) for a total of four sets.*

bod **squad**

These moves will give you the rockin' body of a cheerleader. And as for that short skirt you've been hesitant to wear? Bring it on!

Anyone who says cheerleading isn't a sport hasn't been to a conditioning session! Cheerleaders have to be amazingly fit to do everything from flipping to hoisting each other up in the air. We think they're pretty fly (get it?!). So we asked celebrity choreographer Tony Gonzalez (he choreographed two of the super popular *Bring it On* movies) to create these moves that will strengthen and define your whole body. In about a month, you'll feel stronger and have more energy.

- You need a pair of 3–5 lb. weights or two full 12 oz. water bottles.
- First get your heart pumping by running in place for two minutes.
- When you've finished the moves, walk for 10 minutes to cool down. Then do the stretch pictured at the end of the workout.
- Do the moves in the order they're shown, three times a week. By the first day of school, you'll look hot!

x-out

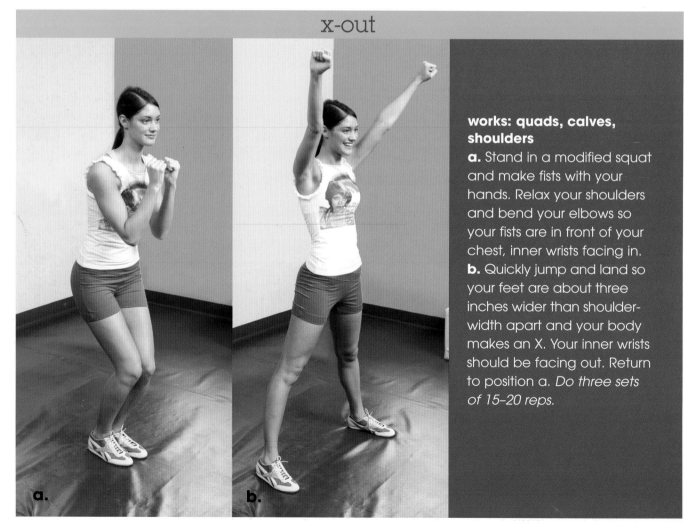

works: quads, calves, shoulders
a. Stand in a modified squat and make fists with your hands. Relax your shoulders and bend your elbows so your fists are in front of your chest, inner wrists facing in.
b. Quickly jump and land so your feet are about three inches wider than shoulder-width apart and your body makes an X. Your inner wrists should be facing out. Return to position a. *Do three sets of 15–20 reps.*

a.

b.

push-up

a.

b.

works: triceps, biceps, chest, abs
a. Get in a push-up position. Place your index fingers and thumbs together to form a triangle directly below your neck. Lift your right leg about 10–12 inches above the ground.
b. Keeping your abs tight so your body is in a straight line, bend your arms to lower your body as far as you can, then return to position a. (Too hard? Leave both feet on the floor, then work up to lifting your leg.) *Do 10, switch legs and repeat.*

no! don't let your hips drop or lift your raised leg too high—you could strain your back.

no!

upright row

a.

b.

works: upper back, shoulders, biceps
a. Stand with your feet together, knees bent, holding the weights in front of you.
b. Keeping your hands in the same position, bend your elbows to "pull" the weights up toward your chin, forming a half V. Return to position a. *Do three sets of eight reps.*

candlestick

a.

b.

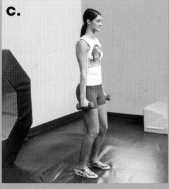
c.

d.

works: shoulders, biceps

a. Stand with your knees slightly bent, holding the weights or water bottles at the sides of your body.

b. Slowly raise your arms in front of you to shoulder height, holding weights vertically. Hold for five seconds.

c. Return to position a.

d. Raise your arms out to the sides, palms facing forward, to shoulder height so your body forms a T. Hold for five seconds, then return to position a. *Do three sets of 15 reps.*

v-up

a.

b.

works: abs

a. Lie on your back with your legs and arms extended.

b. Squeeze your abs as you slowly raise your upper body and legs, opening them into a V. Thrust your hands forward through your legs, keeping your toes pointed and your back straight. Slowly return to position a. *Do three sets of eight reps.*

arm stretch

post workout

Always stretch after using weights to prevent injury. Straighten your right arm. Hook your left elbow in front as you pull your right arm across your body. Hold for 10 seconds. You'll feel it in your shoulder. *Repeat on your left arm. Ahhhhh!*

hit like a girl!

Kickboxing tones your arms, abs, butt, and legs. Plus, it's great for relieving stress. So get ready to kick some, um, air!

Do you ever get so stressed out that you just want to, you know, hit something? Here's your chance! Jeff Harper, a kickboxing instructor at The Sports Club/L.A. in New York City, says that shadowboxing (punching and kicking the air) relieves stress and is a great cardio workout.

Get started: Warm up by jogging or jumping rope for five minutes, then do all four of these moves two times in a row. Walk for five minutes to cool down, then stretch your neck, arms, back, and legs. (The entire workout takes about 25 minutes.) Do it three times a week and you'll look and feel stronger in about four weeks—before your winter vacation is over!

jab

a.   **b.**

works: shoulders, back, and arms
a. Stand with knees slightly bent and feet shoulder-width apart, your left heel even with the toes of your right foot. Picture 12 o'clock in front of you, then turn your hips to 2 o'clock. Hold fists in front of your chin, keeping elbows in.
b. Keeping right fist near chin, throw a left punch at shoulder level as quickly as you can. (Don't overextend your arm!) Immediately return to starting position. *Alternate doing 10 left jabs, then 10 right jabs (put right foot forward) for two minutes.*

roundhouse kick

a.

b.

works: legs, butt, and abs

a. Stand with knees slightly bent and feet shoulder-width apart, right heel even with the toes of your left foot. Turn hips to 10 o'clock. Make fists as you did for the jab and imagine you are about to kick the side of a punching bag.
b. In one continuous motion, lift left leg to hip level and whip it around the right side of your body. As you kick, pivot on right foot and rotate your hips to the right. You should end up with your left shoulder pointing toward your imaginary target. Return to the starting position. *Alternate 10 left kicks with 10 right kicks (whipping right leg as you pivot on your left foot) for two minutes.*

cross punch

a.

b.

works: shoulders, arms, and abs

a. Get into the same starting position as for the jab.
b. Keeping your left fist in front of your chin, twist and punch your right arm across your body at shoulder level (imagine you are aiming for a punching bag in front of your left shoulder). As you punch, pivot on your right foot so your right heel moves out and away from your body. *Alternate doing 10 right cross punches, then 10 left cross punches (put your right foot forward) for two minutes.*

knee jab

a.

b.

works: legs, butt, and abs

a. Stand with knees slightly bent and feet shoulder-width apart, your left heel even with the toes of your right foot. Make loose fists; extend arms in front of you at shoulder level. Turn your hips to 2 o'clock.
b. Quickly raise your right knee as high as you can while rising up on the ball of your left foot. As you knee, pull your hands in toward your body. Quickly return to the starting position. Alternate left knee jabs and right knee jabs for two minutes.
Once you've completed moves 1–4, return to move 1 and repeat each one more time.

the reggaeton **workout**

It's easy to tone your arms, legs, back, and butt—just shake 'em with this routine done to a fusion of Latin, reggae, and hip-hop.

You've probably heard the thump of the "Dem Bow" beat—bum...ba bum ba—blairing in a club or at the beach. That's reggaeton, a sexy sound from Puerto Rico. Choreographer Melanie Aguirre created these moves just for you to do to a reggaeton beat. Just hold each position for one count (a count in one beat of music). Once you get the hang of the moves, combine them in the order they're shown and repeat the whole routine to at least two songs every day—working up to five or more songs for a more challenging workout. Uno, dos, tres— vámanos! (One, two, three—let's go!)

dip and roll

works: arms and thighs

a. Stand with your knees bent, your feet slightly more than shoulder-width apart, and your left knee turned inward. Lean your torso down toward your right side. Start rolling your arms around each other disco-style, keeping your forearms parallel to the ground.

b. Continue rolling as you straighten your legs and torso.

c. Keep rolling as you lean down toward your left side with your right knee turned inward. *Try to keep in time with the music by changing position with each beat. Do four sets (a+b+c=one set), rest for 10 seconds, then repeat.*

a. **b.** **c.**

squat snap

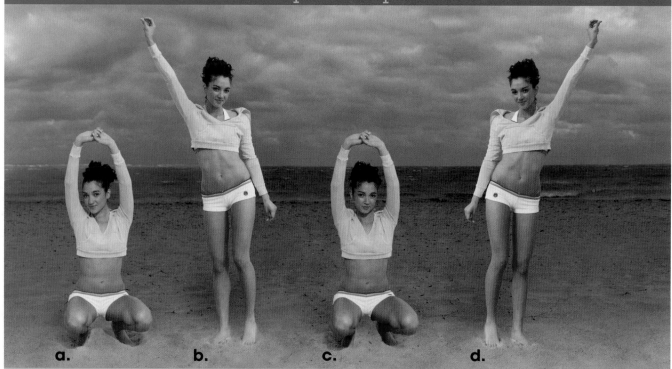

a. **b.** **c.** **d.**

works: butt, thighs, calves, and shoulders

a. Squat so you're balancing on the balls of your feet, with your butt resting on your heels. Raise your arms over your head (palms facing up) and clasp your fingertips together.

b. "Snap" up to standing position, swinging your hips to the left, lowering your left arm, and snapping your fingers on both hands.

c. Return to starting position.

d. Repeat step b, but this time swing your hips to the right and lower your right arm.

Do four sets (a+b+c+d=one set).

the genie

works: obliques and thighs

a. Stand with your feet together and knees slightly bent. Hold your arms at shoulder-level with your elbows bent so your fists face each other. Swing your hips to the right.

b. Keeping your knees bent, swing your hips to the left in one motion. Repeat, going back and forth to the beat, keeping your arms level. Each hip swing is one count. *Do two sets of eight, rest for 10 seconds, then do two more sets.*

a.   b.

row pull

works: upper back, obliques, and thighs

a. Stand with your feet shoulder-width apart, and turn your hips slightly to the left. Raise your arms over your head and grasp your left wrist with your right hand.

b. Keeping your right foot flexed, lift it up so your knee is turned in and your shin is parallel to the ground. Simultaneously swing your arms to the right. Alternate back and forth between your right and left sides four times. *Do two sets, rest, then do two more sets.*

a.   b.

toning moves for every area

weight machine **101**

Come with us to the gym and learn how to use all those intimidating weight machines. Then feel free to grunt all you want!

Treadmills and stair-climbers are easy enough to use…but weight machines? Not so much! Figuring them out can be difficult (even for trainers) and sometimes embarrassing! We asked Cindy Sherwin and Bethani Lown, certified trainers at The Gym in New York City, to explain the correct way to use the five most common weight machines.

For each exercise shown here, start with 2 or 3 sets of 12–15 reps. The weight should be heavy enough that you feel resistance but you're not straining. If 15 reps is too easy, add weight. If you can't get past 6 reps, take off weight until you can complete 3 sets.
Don't let the weights clang together between reps. Instead, lower them with control—it forces you to keep your muscles flexed.

the fly

a. **b.**

works: chest
a. Adjust the seat so that your hands are slightly lower than your shoulders when you grab the handles.
b. Sit tall with your chest out a tiny bit and slowly pull the handles to meet each other without locking your elbows. *Your return motion should take a slow count of "1, 2, 3."*

bicep curl

a.

b.

works: upper arms

a. Sit down and adjust the height of the seat so you're leaning forward and your armpits are resting on the top of the pad. Grasp the handles from underneath so your forearms are facing up and your wrists are shoulder-width apart.
b. Contract your abs, then pull the bar toward you on a slow count of "1, 2, 3" until your fists are a foot in front your nose. As you curl, keep your wrists aligned with your forearms— don't let them bend backward. *Slowly return to position a.*

ab crunch

a.

b.

works: abs

a. Adjust the seat so the lower parts of your shins rest against the pads and you don't have to reach any higher than the top of your head for the handles when you're seated. Relax your shoulders and grab the handles so your elbows are even and pointing forward.
b. Tuck your chin slightly and crunch forward by squeezing your ab muscles. (Your back should round out like a cat's.) *Relax your ab muscles and return to position a. If your neck felt strained, lighten the weight one level.*

lat pull

a.

b.

works: upper back
a. Sit down and adjust the knee pad so that it's an inch above your knees. Then stand up and grasp the bar with your hands shoulder-width apart. Keeping your arms straight, pull the bar down as you sit. Your feet should be forward, your back straight (or slightly angled back), and your focus directly in front of you.
b. Pull the bar down in front of your face and toward your collarbone on a 3-second count. Keep your elbows tucked close to your body. *Slowly raise your arms (counting "1, 2, 3") to return to position a without locking your elbows.*

no! Don't pull the bar behind your head.

leg press

works: butt, quads, and hamstrings

a. Lie back on the bench, place your feet hip-width apart in the middle of the platform, and bend your knees 90 degrees.

b. Push through your heels (not your toes) as you slowly count "1, 2, 3" to extend your legs without locking our knees. *Count to 3 as you return to start.*

training day

Try to choose a machine in front of a mirror so you can check that your form is correct—and admire how toned you're looking! Don't be afraid to ask a gym employee how to use a machine properly. That's what they're there for!

If you can't find these exact machines at your gym, ask a trainer who works there to show you a similar machine that will work the same muscles or similar muscle groups.

hard **core**

Want to make your stomach flatter and posture better? Try this core-strengthening workout!

The muscles that make up your core—your abs, obliques, and lower back muscles—provide power for all your movements. When you strengthen your core, your posture improves and all your other muscles work more efficiently, which helps prevent injuries from sports and other exercises. Bonus: Having a strong core is the first step to getting the oh-so-sexy six-pack! So do this routing created by New York City trainer Les James four or five times a week (it takes 20 minutes) and you'll see results in four weeks. It's pretty tough, so you might be a little sore the first week. But you can handle it—you're *hard core*!

fab ab tips

- During all these moves, keep your abs engaged (pulled in tight and contracted). To get an idea of what it feels like, stand up, place your palms on your stomach, and cough. Feel that tightening? That's what your abs should feel like when you use them to do these moves.
- For each set, do as many reps as you can while maintaining the correct form. We suggest 10–15 reps, but your number may be different for each move.

twisting sit-up

works: abs, obliques, and lower back

a. Lie on your back with your hands behind your head, elbows out. Bend your right knee so your right foot is on the floor and extend your left leg out straight, holding it about 4 inches off the floor.

b. Use your abs to pull your body into a sit-up position as you twist your torso and bend your left leg, bringing your right elbow to your left knee at the top of the sit-up. Slowly recline back to the starting position without letting your left leg touch the floor. *Do 10–15 reps, then switch sides and repeat. Do 3 sets.*

a. b.

calypso leg circles

a. b. c.

works: abs, lower back, and quads

a. Lie on your back and grasp the legs of a chair placed behind your head. Keeping your lower back pressed to the floor, raise your legs until they're perpendicular to the floor.

b. With your lower back still pressed to the ground, trace half circles in the air with your toes in a smooth, continuous motion.

(Imagine your right toes tracing the right side of a circle and your left toes tracing the left side.)

c. Complete your half circles by bringing your legs together about 4 inches off the ground. Keeping your legs together, raise them back into the starting position. *Do 3 sets of 10 or more leg circles.*

superman

works: butt, lower back, and upper back

a. Lie on your stomach, arms and legs extended. Keeping your chin touching the floor, raise your left arm and right leg at the same time until they are about 6 inches above the floor, then lower them.

b. Raise your right arm and left leg the same way. *Do 3 sets of 10 reps (raising one side and then the other side counts as one rep).*

no! Don't lift your chin. Keep it on the floor.

a.

b.

les's special sit-up

works: abs and lower back

a. Lie on your back, knees bent, feet flat on the floor. Extend your arms so your fingers point to the ceiling.

b. Keeping your arms perpendicular to the floor, use your abs to pull your body into a sit-up position. It's okay if your feet lift up—but keep your hands pointing to the ceiling. Return to position a. *Do 3 sets of 10 or more sit-ups.*

no! Don't reach your arms in front of your body as you sit up.

a.

b.

bonus!

1-minute move
Lie as shown. Keeping your lower back pressed to the floor, hold the position for 1 minute. When you feel the quiver in your abs, you know it's working!

side plank extension

no!

works: back, abs, obliques, butt, and quads

a. On your left side with your legs together, support your weight with your left foot and left forearm so your body forms a straight line from your feet to the top of your head. Point your right fingers to the ceiling.
b. Hold the side plank as you raise your right leg until it's

parallel to the floor. Return to position a. *Hold the side plank as you do 10 leg lifts. Switch sides and do 10 more lifts. Repeat the entire set two more times.*

no! Don't let your hips drop toward the floor.

a.

b.

ab **fabulous!**

Want rock-solid abs? These four easy moves will strengthen your abs in less than 10 minutes a day!

With some cardio of your own and these moves from the *Basic Ab Workout for Dummies* video, you can get a washboard stomach. We asked Gay Gasper, the trainer who stars in the video, to design a tummy-toning workout to strengthen the muscles in your midsection. Do all four exercises every day (it takes about 10 minutes) to see results in about two weeks.

slow-speed bicycle

a.

b.

works: your obliques (muscles along the sides of your torso)

a. Lie on your back and place your hands gently behind your head with your elbows pointing out. Using your ab muscles, lift your head and neck off the floor and pull both of your knees toward your belly, keeping your lower back pressed against the floor. To begin the bicycling movement, extend your right leg until it's almost straight and your foot is about 2 feet above the floor, then twist your torso and touch your right elbow to your left knee. Hold the position (shown above) for 2 seconds.
b. Now pull your right knee back toward your belly as you extend your left leg and twist your torso to touch your left elbow to your right knee. Hold the position for 2 seconds, then switch. *Do 2 sets of 20 reps.*

no!
Keep your elbows out and don't pull on the back of your head.

no!

scissors

a.

b.

works: your upper and lower abs

a. Lie on your back with hands placed under your hips, palms on the floor. Raise both legs off the floor until they form an L with your body. Slowly lower your left leg until it's about 2 inches above the floor.

b. Return your left leg to the starting position as you lower your right leg until it's 2 inches above the floor. (Your legs should look like a big pair of scissors opening and closing.) *Do 2 sets of 20 reps without pausing between reps.*

CG! tip: Don't use momentum to swing your legs up and down. Contract your ab muscles to slowly raise and lower your legs.

toe dips

a.

b.

works: lower abs

a. Lie with elbows out and hands behind your head, then raise your shoulders off the floor. (Don't tuck your chin!) With toes pointed, lift your legs and bend your knees so your calves are parallel to the floor.

b. Lower your left foot until your toes are just above the floor but not touching it (hold for 5 seconds). Return left leg to starting position, then repeat with right leg (hold for 2 seconds). *Do 2 sets of 20 reps.*

a.   b.   c.

boxing **babe**

Get your arms, legs and butt buff with kickboxing!

Put on some medium-paced music and do this series of moves (a–d) for 3 minutes on each side. Start with your right side, then do on your left (jab with your left arm, cross right, and kick left). Try 5 sets (doing the moves on both sides equals 1 set) 4–5 times a week.

a. stance: Stand with feet 1 foot apart, right foot forward, fists in front of your chest.
b. jab: Punch right arm straight out in front of your body (don't lock your elbow).
c. cross: Punch left arm straight out while pivoting left foot inward.
d. front kick: Kick your right leg to a right angle (as if aiming for someone's stomach).

jump! jump!

When you're ready to add intensity to your kickboxing workout, get your heart pumping by jumping rope for 3 minutes after completing each side.

d.

work out in **bed!**

Can't stand getting up to exercise? With these moves, you can tone your arms, abs, and legs before you even brush your teeth!

Getting out of bed in the morning can be tough, let alone getting up even earlier to exercise! But what if you could work out in your pj's without even leaving your room? We asked trainer Kimberly Garrison, owner of 1 on 1 Ultimate Fitness in Philadelphia, to create this easy routine of four moves. Do them four times a week (they only take 15 minutes) and you'll strengthen your arms, abs, and legs. You'll not only be able to sneak in a workout, you'll also get a rush of endorphins that'll put you in a good mood to face the day. That's enough to turn anyone into a morning person!

leg lift

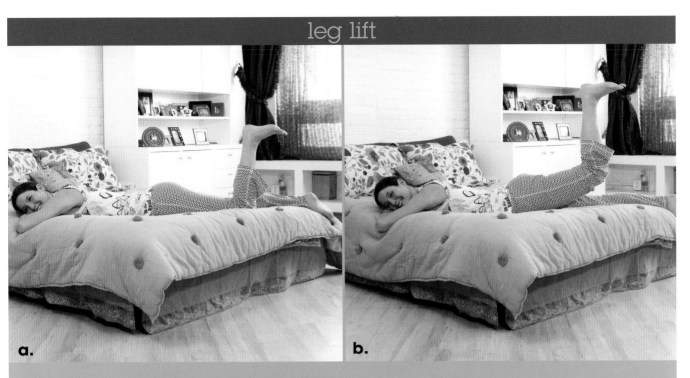

a.

b.

works: your butt and the backs of your thighs

a. Lie on your stomach on your bed with arms crossed and your head resting on your hands. Bend left knee so your leg forms a 90-degree angle, and flex left foot so the bottom of foot is parallel to the ceiling.

b. Keeping the bottom of your left foot parallel to the ceiling, squeeze butt muscles as you raise left knee about a foot off the bed. Return to start. *Do 3 sets of 15 lifts with each leg, alternating between right-leg sets and left-leg sets.*

lat pull-down

a.

b.

works: your shoulders, upper back, and biceps

a. Sit cross-legged on your bed, keeping your back straight and your abs pulled in. Hold a pillowcase or towel above your head with palms facing out and hands placed slightly wider than hip-width apart.

b. Clench your fists (it makes your arm muscles contract), then "pull" (or lower) the towel in front of your body, squeezing your shoulder blades together as you go, until it's about four inches beneath your chin. Return to the starting position. *Do 3 sets of 15 reps.*

crunch

a.

b.

works: your abs

a. Lie on your back on the floor, perpendicular to your bed, then rest your calves on your bed so your legs form a 90-degree angle. (If your bed is too high or low for your legs to form a 90-degree angle, you can use a chair or simply hold your legs at a 90-degree angle in the air.)

Cross your arms over your chest.
b. Exhale as you contract your abs to raise your shoulders about 6 inches off the floor. (Look at the ceiling so you don't tuck your chin.) Return to the starting position. *Do 3 sets of 20 crunches.*

leg pulse

a.

b.

works: the fronts of your thighs
a. Sit on the edge of your bed with your back straight and your abs pulled in. Extend your left leg in front of you so your left heel rests on the floor. (If your bed is lower than 16 inches or higher than 24 inches, sit on a chair instead.)
b. Raise your left leg toward the ceiling until it's parallel to the floor, then "pulse" it by lowering it almost to the floor (but not touching it) and raising it until it's parallel to the floor again. (Each pulse should take about one second.) *Do 3 sets of 15 pulses on each leg, alternating right-leg sets and left-leg sets.*

tennis, **anyone?**

Tones arms, lean legs...get in shape so you can play like a pro—or just look hot in a tennis skirt!

Want to play tennis like a pro? All the power you need comes from your core muscles: your abs, back, and hips. Do these six exercises three days a week to strengthen your core and tone your butt, legs, and shoulders. You'll need an exercise ball and a resistance band as well as a mat or towel to use as padding.

bird dog

a. Get on all fours and tighten your lower abs so that your back is flat. Squeeze your shoulder blades together.
b. Extend right leg behind you and left arm in front of you. Switch sides (extend left leg and right arm), keeping focused on edge of mat. Keep abs tight so hips don't move. *Do 10 on each side; 2 sets total.*

tennis advantage: power for serving and fore- and backhands

shoulder and trunk rotation

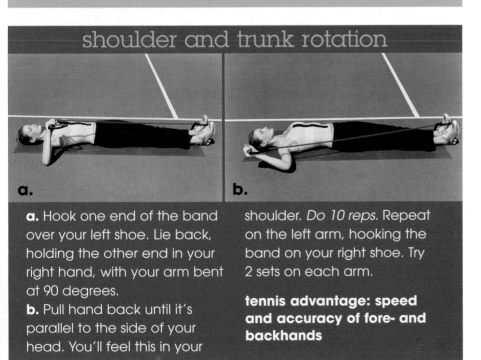

a. Hook one end of the band over your left shoe. Lie back, holding the other end in your right hand, with your arm bent at 90 degrees.
b. Pull hand back until it's parallel to the side of your head. You'll feel this in your shoulder. *Do 10 reps.* Repeat on the left arm, hooking the band on your right shoe. Try 2 sets on each arm.

tennis advantage: speed and accuracy of fore- and backhands

dead bug

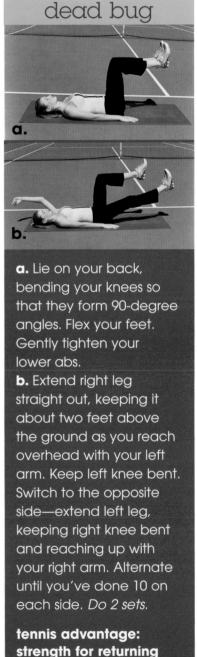

a. Lie on your back, bending your knees so that they form 90-degree angles. Flex your feet. Gently tighten your lower abs.
b. Extend right leg straight out, keeping it about two feet above the ground as you reach overhead with your left arm. Keep left knee bent. Switch to the opposite side—extend left leg, keeping right knee bent and reaching up with your right arm. Alternate until you've done 10 on each side. *Do 2 sets.*

tennis advantage: strength for returning ground strokes

bridge with leg lifts

a. Lie on your back with calves and heels on the ball. Contract your abs and butt. Let your arms rest on the ground at your sides.
b. Slowly lift your hips off the mat without arching your back. Lift left leg off the ball, lower it back onto the ball, then repeat with right leg. Stay balanced by keeping your abs and butt tight. Don't use your arms to help you up. *Do 2 sets of 10 reps each.*

tennis advantage: power for serves and making drop shots

ball squats

a. Stand against a wall with the ball behind you, feet shoulder-width apart and about a foot in front of you.
b. Squat so your legs are at a 90-degree angle. Keep knees over ankles and abs tight. Return to starting position. *Do 2 sets of 10.*

tennis advantage: speed for running cross-court

ball push-up

a. Start in a kneeling position with the ball under your stomach. Walk your hands out on the ground in front of you until your shins are on the ball and you're in a push-up position. Don't let your back sag; keep abs tight.

b. Bend arms and do a push-up, stopping about 6 inches from the ground. *Try 2 sets of 10 reps.*

tennis advantage: racquet speed; accuracy of volleys and fore-and backhands

legs **go!**

You'll really strut your stuff in that mini once you do these leg-toning moves!

Equinox Fitness Club's celebrity personal trainer Kacy Duke suggests doing these exercises to strengthen and shape your legs. They'll work your heart too. You'll need an 8–10-pound weight (or a 3-liter bottle of water) and a chair. Before doing the moves below, warm up and work your other muscles by jumping rope for a minute and doing 8–10 push-ups or sit-ups—try 10 sets. Do this workout 2–3 days a week. Your legs may be sore after the first time, but don't let that stop you—just take a day off before doing it again.

plié drag

a.

b.

works: inner thighs

a. Stand with feet slightly wider than hip distance apart and turned out at 45 degrees—like second position in ballet. Place your hands on hips. Bend your legs so you're almost in a squat, but keep your back straight and don't stick out your butt.

b. Now drag your right foot along the ground toward your left, so that your heels come together as you straighten your legs. You should feel this in your inner thighs. If you don't, press more weight into your right foot as you drag. Repeat with the left leg. *Do 12 reps on each side. Work up to 3 sets total.*

knee lift & back lunge

a. **b.**

works: quadriceps, hamstrings
a. Stand next to a chair with the back of the chair next to the right side of your body. Hold on to the chair for balance. Lift your right leg so it's bent at a 90-degree angle and even with your hip.
b. Swing your right leg back into a deep lunge position, so your back leg is bent as close to 90 degrees as possible, with the ball of your foot on the ground (heel lifted). Your left leg should form a 90-degree angle, so your left knee is directly over your ankle. Return to starting position. *Do 12 lifts and lunges on each side. Work up to 3 sets.*

side lunge

a. **b.**

works: butt, upper hamstrings, inner thighs
a. Stand with legs spread as wide as they'll comfortably go, knees straight but not locked, with your feet turned out to 45 degrees. Hold the weight (or bottle of water) with both hands in front of your body.
b. Keeping your chest lifted, bend your left leg into a lunge as you reach toward your left toes and place the weight on the ground. Let go of the weight for a second, then pick it up and slowly return to starting position, squeezing your butt as you go. Repeat with your right leg. *Do 12 lunges on each side, alternating sides. Work up to 3 sets.*

jump squat

a. **b.**

works: all leg muscles, heart
a. Start in a standing position with feet together. Then clasp your hands in front of your body and squat down like you're about to sit in a chair. Keep your back straight.
b. Jump up, reaching toward the sky with arms and legs spread, so that your body forms an X shape in the air. It should feel like a burst of energy and look like a cheerleading jump. Land in the starting position, making sure you bend your knees as you land to cushion the shock and protect your knees from injury. Then repeat the jump in quick succession 12 times. *Work up to 3 sets of 12, resting for a few seconds between each set.*

the snowboard workout

Pro-boarding trainer Dee Tidwell created this winter-sports workout that'll give your butt a serious boost!

Dee Tidwell helps pro snowboarders stay in awesome shape year-round with exercises that really challenge their core and lower-body strength and balance. You can get *your* body ready for snowboarding (or just get stronger and more fit) by doing this routine three or four days a week. Be sure to take one day off in between workouts. Use your off days to do cardiovascular exercise—run, bike, or climb stairs for 45 minutes. That's what you call a well-rounded program!

prone cobra

works: upper, mid- and lower back, glutes

a. Lie facedown, arms at your sides with your palms flat on the ground. You should be looking at the ground during the entire exercise.

b. Arch your upper body off the ground and stretch your arms back behind you, with palms facing outward and thumbs pointing toward the sky. Squeeze your butt and pull shoulder blades back. Hold for 20 seconds; release and relax for 20 seconds. Repeat 9 times. Your goal is to hold the pose for 3 minutes *without* resting, so build up to that by holding for 10 more seconds every time the move gets too easy.

lateral ball roll

works: hamstrings, glutes, lower back, mid-back, shoulders

a. Let shoulders and head rest on a medium-sized exercise ball. Legs should be at 90-degree angles with feet on the ground, hip-width apart. Look at the sky and stretch your arms out to the side, palms facing up. Keep your abs tight and your pelvis tucked throughout the exercise.

b. Slowly inch your feet and slide your upper body to the left until it's halfway off the ball. Anchor your right shoulder to the ball by using your back and leg muscles. Keep pressure on your heels and squeeze your butt so you don't lose your balance. (Hips should stay parallel to the ground.) Hold for 2 seconds; roll back to start position. Repeat by sliding your body to the right. *Do 6–10 times, alternating sides. Rest for 60 seconds, and repeat the series twice more.*

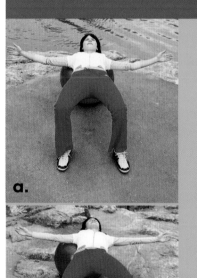

multidirectional lunge

works: abs, obliques, lower back, glutes, hip flexors, hamstrings, quads, inner thighs, calves

a. Step into a lunge with your right foot in front. Bend both knees so legs form 90-degree angles. To prevent injury, make sure your right kneecap doesn't extend past your toes. Return to standing position.

b. Step your right foot out again, but this time step slightly to the right (clockwise), then bend both knees so your legs form 90-degree angles. Return to standing.

c. Step right foot out to the side and bend only that knee (left leg stays straight). Return to standing.

d. Step right foot back at an angle. Bend knees until each leg forms a 90-degree angle. Return to standing.

e. Copy a, but this time, place your right foot behind instead of in front of you. Return to standing. Repeat each move with left leg, starting with e and ending with a. *Do 1–3 sets.*

boarding tips from a pro rider

• Stick with it! Your first three days are hard. You'll be bruised and sore, but it does get easier and more fun.

• When you fall, try to land on your bottom. If you fall forward with arms out to catch yourself, you could get hurt.

• Wear butt pads to reduce soreness, and when you're just learning, prevent injury with a helmet and wrist pads.

hip extension

works: hamstrings, abs, obliques, glutes, lower back

a. Lie on the ground with both of your heels resting on the top middle section of the exercise ball. Your arms should be at your sides, with elbows bent and your fists pointing upward.
Look up throughout the entire exercise, and make sure that you keep your head and neck relaxed on the ground.

b. Slowly lift hips off the ground as high as you can by squeezing your butt and pressing heels into the ball. Pause for 1 second, balancing on arms and shoulder blades, and slowly release. Keep your abs tight and pelvis tucked throughout the move (your body should create a straight line from your stomach to your pelvis). *Do 1–3 sets (8–15 reps per set), resting 60 seconds in between.*

get a celebrity
body!

Ever look at a celebrity and think, I wish I could have that body? Try these mini workouts from the trainers who get Jennifer Aniston, Jessica Alba, and Beyoncé in shape!

We asked you who had the best body in Hollywood, and guess what? One celeb didn't win it—instead you picked a combo of Jennifer Aniston's sculpted arms, Jessica Alba's killer abs, and Beyoncé's toned butt and legs. Well, you can have them all—it just takes a good routine and dedication. We asked Jennifer's, Jessica's, and Beyoncé's trainers to create three mini workouts based on their clients' intense routines. Do all three for a 40-minute full-body workout every other day, or work one body part each day. You should begin to see results in about three weeks. So don't be surprised if the paparazzi start snapping photos of you next time you're at the beach!

get Jen's arms

Jen tones her arms and shoulders with Budokon, a blend of yoga and martial arts invented by Cameron Shayne. He says the Budokon moves on the next page tone your entire body, especially your arms. In a slow, continuous motion, flow through the positions of each move, then repeat the entire workout twice. It takes about 15 minutes altogether.

modified dancing dog

works: triceps, biceps, and shoulders

To do the move, work through the following positions in a smooth, continuous motion.

a. Stand with your feet shoulder-width apart, then bend over and place your hands palms-down on the ground so your body forms an upside-down V.

b. Keeping your right leg straight, raise it behind you until it's about 3 feet above the ground.

c. Bend your right knee to fold your right heel toward your butt.

d. Keeping your left hand planted on the ground, raise your right arm. Now begin to drop your right foot behind your body by twisting your torso to your right.

e. Continue twisting and raising your arm until you can place your right foot on the ground behind your left leg and your right arm is fully extended above your body. Reverse back through the move to return to the starting position. *Do 3 reps (steps a-e) on each side.*

single-leg sweep

works: triceps, biceps, and shoulders

a. Stand with your feet about three feet apart, then bend over and place the palm of your right hand on the ground, angled to the left.

b. Lift your right foot off the ground and begin to turn to your left by pivoting on your left foot.

c. Continue pivoting on your left foot as you bring your right leg in front of your left leg.

d. Keeping your weight balanced on your right hand, continue pivoting until your left foot is pointing left and your right leg is fully extended. Slowly reverse back through the move to return to the starting position. *Do 3 reps (steps a-d) on each side.*

get Beyoncé's butt

This workout by trainer Mark Jenkins includes the toning moves he has done with Beyoncé. You can turn it into a calorie-burning cardio workout by jumping rope for five minutes before you begin, then doing 100 skips of a jump rope between moves. Including cardio, the workout takes about 20 minutes.

reverse lunge

a.

b.

works: thighs and butt
a. Stand with your feet about shoulder-width apart and your arms at your sides, holding a 3-pound weight or full 20-ounce water bottle in each hand.
b. Keeping your back straight, step back with your right foot about three feet and dip your right knee until it is only an inch or two above the ground. Your left thigh should be parallel to the ground. Push off with your right foot to return to the starting position. *Do 3 sets of 15 reps, then switch sides and repeat.*

reverse kick

a.   **b.**

works: thighs, hips, and butt
a. Stand 18 inches from a wall. Place your right hand about two feet above your left hand on the wall. Raise your right leg so your knee forms a 90-degree angle and your thigh is parallel to the ground.
b. Squeeze your butt muscle as you push your foot out to straighten your right leg, then pull in your right knee to return to the starting position. *Do 3 sets of 15 slow kicks on each leg.*

pulsing squat

a.   **b.**

works: thighs and butt
a. With your elbows bent and holding your hands palms-together at chin level, lower your butt (as if you were about to sit on a chair) to get into proper squat position. Your thighs should be parallel to the ground.
b. Pulse up and down in a smooth motion by using your butt and thigh muscles to raise your butt about 4 inches, then lower it back to the starting position. *Do 3 sets of 15 reps.*

get Jessica's abs

Trainer Ramona Braganza does this workout with Jessica to tone her upper and lower abs as well as her obliques, which are the muscles on the sides of the waist. Do all three moves without pausing, then go through all three moves two more times. The entire workout takes about 10 to 15 minutes.

roll up

a.　b.

works: upper and lower abs
a. Lie with your knees bent, feet flat on the ground, and arms extended at your sides with your palms down.
b. Contract your abs to roll your torso into a seated position with your arms extended parallel to the ground. Return to the starting position. The pace for each rep is two seconds to roll up, two seconds to roll down. *Do 10 reps.*

plank

a.

b.

works: arms, abs, and lower back
a. Get into a push-up position with your forearms on the ground so your body forms a straight line from shoulders to heels. Keeping your abs pulled in, raise your right foot off the ground 6 inches. Hold the position for 10 seconds.
b. Return your right foot to the ground, then raise your left foot. Hold for 10 seconds. Rest, repeat. *Do 3 reps.*

bicycle

works: abs and obliques
a. Lie with your hands behind your head, then contract your abs to bring your head and neck off the floor. Begin cycling by extending your right leg as you bring your left knee and right elbow together.
b. Continue cycling by twisting your torso to reach your left elbow toward your right knee. Bicycle in a smooth motion for 20 reps (left knee then right knee = one rep).

a.　b.

hoop, here it **is!**

Get yourself a hoop and loosen up—literally! This workout stretches your muscles, tones your core, and puts you in a carefree summer mood now.

Do your neck and shoulders ever feel tight? You need to relax—and we found a new way to help you do it! Hooping relieves tension, improves flexibility, and tones your midsection, making it the perfect activity! Here, Loren Bidner—a hooping expert and creator of the Actionhoop— teaches you four basic moves. For best results, he suggests using an Actionhoop, which is bigger (so stretching is more comfortable) and heavier (so it's easier to keep in rotation) than the hoops they have at toy stores. Do the moves three times in a row every other day (it takes about 30 minutes), and you'll be relaxed and fit!

backward steering

stretches: upper arms, sides of your waist, and back

a. Stand with feet shoulder-width apart. Hold the hoop at 3 o'clock and 9 o'clock, about a foot behind you. Push your chest out and try to squeeze your shoulder blades together.

b. Turn the hoop clockwise until your left hand is directly above your head and your right hand is behind your butt. Hold for 10 seconds; take slow, deep breaths as your muscles stretch.

c. Return to the starting position, then turn the hoop counterclockwise so your right hand is directly above your head and your left hand is behind your butt. Hold for 10 seconds.

forward bend

stretches: spine, arms, shoulders
a. Stand with your feet shoulder-width apart. Hold the hoop at 10 o'clock and 2 o'clock so it's in front of your toes. Bend your knees to lower your butt about 4 inches.

b. Using the hoop for resistance, bend from the waist and straighten your arms. (You'll feel your shoulders stretching.) Bend farther so your torso almost touches your thighs, then stretch your arms all the way in front of you and imagine your spine lengthening. Take slow, deep breaths and relax your neck so your head hangs toward the ground. Hold for 10 seconds and come up slowly.

twists

stretches: abs, shoulders, back
a. Start in the same position as you did for backward steering. Keeping your toes pointing forward and your head in a straight line with your spine, twist from the waist until your chest and head are facing to your right. Hold for 10 seconds and breathe deeply as your muscles stretch.

b. Slowly return to the starting position. Repeat the move on the other side (so your chest and head are facing to your left). Hold for 10 seconds. After you finish the stretching moves, shake out your body, relax, and move on to hooping (page 101).

right

wrong

tones: abs, obliques
strengthens: lower back
a. Keep your shoulders, chest, and head calm and still. Keep your knees soft (not locked).
wrong
Don't look down at the hoop. (You'll mess up your rhythm!)
Don't bend your waist or make exaggerated movements.
Don't wiggle your knees wildly.
Hold the hoop against your lower back, then spin it left or right (whichever feels comfortable) and begin making small, gentle circles with your pelvis until you find a rhythm that keeps the hoop spinning. Next place your hands on your head (this stabilizes your upper body and helps you isolate the muscles in your core). Hoop for 3 minutes. Stop and hoop in the other direction for 3 more minutes.

CG! tip: Have trouble keeping the hoop up? Put on music—the rhythm helps! Return to the first move and repeat the entire workout two more times.

cg! challenge: the lasso

tones: biceps and triceps
Grab the hoop behind your head like it's a baseball you're about to throw. Make a wide throwing motion out to the side (rather than over your head), release your grip on the hoop, and make a small circular motion with your hand (like you're lassoing). Each time the hoop comes around your hand, grasp and release again. Once it starts to lasso, open your palm so the hoop spins around it. Lasso for 1 minute; repeat with other hand.

workouts for all occasions

shape **up!**

Fitness expert and celeb trainer Kathy Kaehler has created this intense four-month plan to turn you into a stronger, sleeker, more energetic version of yourself by spring. Start with the December plan—then update each month. It's not easy, but you'll feel like a superstar!

december

the plan: 15- to 10-minute workout 3 days a week

get this: A mat (or a fluffy towel), an empty wall, some masking tape, and a tennis ball.

warm-up: To get your heart rate really pumping, walk (like you do when you're running really late) around your house (inside or outside, your choice) for 5 minutes (bonus points for climbing stairs.

the workout: These six moves will work your whole body (you may even be a little sore the first week). To prevent injury, always stretch for a few minutes both before and after you work out.

a. Start by doing 30 single-bounce jumping jacks. Remember the ones you used to do in third-grade gym class (in-out, in-out, in-out)? Like that.
b. Now stand against the wall. Slide down until your knees are in line with your ankles and level with your hips (like you're sitting). Hold for 60 seconds.
c. Slide back up, step away from the wall, and turn sideways. Jump up to stick some tape to the wall 2 feet above your head. Now turn sideways and jump up 20 times to smack it. Repeat on the other side.
d. Now face the wall (standing about 2 feet from it), and place your hands on the wall, shoulder-width apart. Lower yourself—like you're doing a push-up—then press back. Repeat 15 times. *Now go back to the jumping jacks and repeat moves a through d.*
e. Great job! Now lie down on your mat with bent knees. Put the tennis ball between your knees, place your hands behind your head, and squeeze your knees and butt together. Repeat 25 times slowly (a and b and c) then 25 times *quickly* (a 'n' b 'n' c 'n' …). Now continue the *slow* knee squeezes for another 25 reps, but each time you squeeze the tennis ball, your shoulder blades off the floor and do a stomach crunch (be sure not to arch your back).

chow, bella!
Nodding off in your afternoon classes? To stay energized, eat a fruit or veggie in each of these colors (that's five total) throughout the day: yellow, red, green, orange, and purple.

the plan: 25- to 30-minute workout 3 to 4 days a week.

get this: Two 5-pound weights (at most sporting goods stores for about $14) and a sturdy chair.

warm-up: Walk quickly around your house for about 5 minutes.

the workout: Do a–d (left), then f–i (below). Repeat a–d, f–i, and finish with e–f (left), upping your reps from 25 to 30.

f. Grab the weights and sit tall in a chair (arms by your side). Bend your arms, curl the weights to your shoulders, then slowly lower (this works your biceps). *Repeat 15 times.*

g. On the last rep of biceps curls, stop at your shoulders, face your palms forward, and push straight up. Bring the weights back to your shoulders and push up again (this works your shoulders). *Repeat 15 times.*

h. Put a pillow in your lap and lay your chest on it. Lift your arms into a T, then lower (this works your back). *Repeat the arm moves 15 times.*

i. Stay bent over, pull your arms in next to your ribs, and bend your elbows. Extend your arms back (see above). Bend and extend (this works your triceps). *Repeat 15 times.*

chow, bella!

Sweet tooth screaming to be satisfied? Eat 100 sugary calories (a third of a chocolate bar) for a fix that's not too high in calories.

the plan: 45- to 60-minute workout 4 to 5 days a week.

get this: A mat or a fluffy towel.

warm-up: Walk quickly around your house for 5 minutes.

the workout: Replace move a with one of these: Walk 3 miles in under 45 minutes or ride a bike for 30 minutes. Then do moves b–d, f–i (left), repeat both groups, and add j–m (below) to the end.

j. Lie down on your back n the mat and slide your hands under your hips. Pull your knees into your chest until your hips rise off your hands. Slowly lower your feet to the floor. *Repeat 20 times.*

k. Place your hands behind your head. Extend your legs straight up (your toes are pointed at the ceiling) and crunch up until your shoulder blades come all the way off the ground. Slowly lower. *Crunch 20 times.*

l. Put your feet back down on the floor (hands behind your head, knees bent). Now exhale and crunch all the way to your knees (get a partner to help you hold down your feet—or slide them under a couch). Slowly inhale and lower. *Repeat 20 times.*

m. Place your left foot on your right knee, then crunch, twist, and try to touch your right elbow to your left knee—lower. *Do this 20 times, then repeat on the other side.*

chow, bella!

Addicted to caffeine? Drink a glass of water for every cup of coffee or soda you consume. Too much caffeine will make your energy levels see-saw.

the plan: 60- to 70-minute workout 5 days a week (you can do it!)

get this: A jump rope, a sturdy chair, and a mat (or a fluffy towel).

warm-up: Walk quickly around your house for 5 minutes.

the workout: Do n–q (below), then j–m (left), upping the reps from 20 to 30. Forget a–i. From April on use a–q to make new 60-minute plans, 3–5 days a week.

n. Tie the rope around your waist and fast walk for 3 miles. *After each mile (about every 15 minutes), jump rope 200 times.*

o. Now go sit on the chair with your hands next to your butt, fingers forward. Slide your butt off the chair and lower it until your elbows are level with your shoulders. Come back up. *Repeat 20 times.*

p. Lie on a mat in front of the chair, put your heels on the seat, and list your hips off the floor. Now squeeze your butt as tight as possible. Lower down. *Repeat 25 times.*

q. Get up, turn to face the chair, step up with one foot, then bring the second foot up beside it. *Do 25— repeat on the other side.*

chow, bella!

Can't wait another hour until dinner? Spread peanut butter on half of a small bagel (protein plus carbs is filling and nutritious).

but I don't want to!

Not in the mood to work out? Try Kathy's trick. Cut out pictures of women you find hardworking and tape them to your mirror. Now, when you need a boost, imagine being them. Sounds corny—but it works!

the prom dress **workout!**

Got at least four weeks till prom? These moves will tone and strengthen your upper arms, back, shoulders, and abs—all the parts your dress shows off!

Whether you're getting ready for prom or planning ahead for tank top weather, now's the time to start toning your upper arms, back, shoulders, and abs. Certified trainer Ashley Salter (shown here doing the moves) is also a model, so she knows the tricks to looking good. Here, she teaches you exercises to tone those muscles you've been neglecting all winter and strengthen your core. (Having a strong core improves your posture, which makes you look better, especially in pictures!) Do this workout every other day and you'll see definition in four weeks—just in time to show off your new look on prom night!

dip

a.

b.

tones: upper arms
a. Sit on the edge of a low chair or bench and place your hands palms-down next to your hips.
b. Slide your butt off the front of the chair and position yourself with your feet set shoulder-width apart. Keeping your back close to the chair, slowly bend your elbows to lower your butt about 6 inches toward the ground. Straighten your arms to lift your butt so it's level with the chair. *Do 3 sets of 10 dips.*

no!
Don't round your torso, as shown here. Keep your abs tight as you dip so your body will stay straight.
To target your upper arms, keep your elbows pointing straight back (not out to the sides).

no!

flutter kick

tones: upper and lower abs

Lie on your back with your hands palms-down beneath your hips. Look up at the ceiling. (It'll help you keep your head in line with your spine.) Keeping your abs tight and your toes pointed, raise your feet about 6 inches off the ground. Using a scissoring motion, kick your feet up and down rapidly as if you're swimming the backstroke. (Be sure not to let your back arch—keep your abs tight.) *Do this for 3 minutes; alternate kicking for 20 seconds and resting for 10 seconds.*

CG! tip: This move will get easier the more you do it, so eventually increase the time you're kicking from 20 to 30 seconds. Then work up to 45 seconds if you can.

decline push-up

a.

b.

tones: shoulders and chest

a. Get in a push-up position with your legs together and your feet placed on a bench (or other sturdy object) so that the balls of your feet are planted 5 inches away from the front of the bench and your hands are directly beneath your shoulders. (Keep your abs and butt tight.)

b. Bend your elbows until they form 90-degree angles to lower your body closer to the floor, then slowly straighten your arms to return to the starting position. *Do 3 sets of 10 push-ups.*

no!
Don't lock your elbows when your arms straighten.
For the best results, keep your abs tight so your butt doesn't sag and your back doesn't arch!

no!

superman

a.

b.

c.

tones: upper and lower back

a. Lie on your stomach with your toes pointed, arms at your sides, palms and forehead on the floor.

b. Keep your head in line with your spine. (Look at the floor so you don't crane your neck.) Then raise your chest about 5 inches off the floor and your arms about 3 inches (with palms still facing down).

c. Slowly bring your arms out and around you until they're shoulder-width apart in front of you. (You'll look like Superman flying.) Keep your shoulders away from your ears (not hunched) and your arms almost straight. Pause for two seconds, then slowly bring your arms back to your sides and return to the starting position. *Do 10 reps. (Each rep should take about 10 seconds.)*

say cheese!

Here are some tips on how to look great in your prom pictures. You've done the workouts, now learn how to show off your results!

DO

Roll your shoulders back and down about an inch so your arms hang away from your body. It's slimming!

DO

Turn your torso away from the camera; place one foot in front of the other, and rest your weight on your back foot. Pretty!

DON'T

Round your back and slouch your shoulders. That pulls everything down, making you look shorter and stockier than you really are.

DON'T

Face the camera square-on and place your feet apart. That makes your body appear wider than it really is.

prom-ercise!

Define the spots your prom dress exposes in less time than it takes to find the perfect shoes.

No matter what you wear to prom, this workout—from New York City personal trainer Lacey Stone—will sculpt your body so you'll look even better in your dream dress. Just think, if your limo gets a flat, you'll have the muscle power to lift the spare out of the trunk! Get started: Every other day, do three sets of the move designed for your dress. Keep it up and you'll start to look toned in two to three weeks!

To do these moves, use a 6- to 10-pound medicine ball or a full half-gallon water jug.

strappy dress

a. **b.**

the move: squats with tricep extensions

why: Spaghetti straps make your arms the main focus—this will tighten your upper arms in no time. Bonus: It also works your butt and thighs!

a. Stand with your feet shoulder-width apart and your arms fully extended, holding a medicine ball above your head.

b. Lower your butt (like you're going to sit on a chair) while you bend your elbows to lower the ball behind your head. Pause when your thighs make a 45-degree angle (see photo); raise the ball as you return to start. Challenge: Squat to 90 degrees. Your knees should not bend past your toes. *Move up and down slowly for 1 minute (about 20 squats).*

111

halter dress

the move: squat raises

why: A halter draws attention to your shoulders—this move gives them a sexier, chiseled look. Bonus: Your butt and thighs get a workout too!

a. Stand with your feet shoulder-width apart and your arms down, holding the medicine ball in front of you at waist level.

b. Sink back into your heels and lower your butt (like you're going to sit on a chair) while you slowly raise the ball. Keep your arms extended the entire time. Pause when your thighs make a

a.

b.

45-degree angle and you're holding the ball above your head (see photo), then slowly lower it as you return to start. Challenge: Squat to 90 degrees. *Move up and down slowly for 1 minute (about 20 squats).*

clingy dress

a.

b.

c.

the move: ab twists

why: It will tone your abs so they look smooth under clingy fabric.

a. Lie on your back with a medicine ball placed between your knees and your knees pulled in toward your belly. Place your hands palms down at your sides.

b. Contract your abs, then use them to slowly lower the ball to the right until your right knee almost touches the floor and your left hip almost lifts off the floor.

c. Then, in a continuous motion, use your abs to move the ball all the way over to the left side of your body until your right hip almost lifts off the floor. *Slowly rotate your knees back and forth in a continuous motion for 1 minute.*

a.

b.

c.

the move: chest flys

why: It will define your chest and the area near your armpits (yes, you have muscles there!).

a. Lie on your back with your knees bent and your feet flat on the floor. With the medicine ball in your left hand, extend both your arms out to your sides so your body forms a T shape.

b. With your elbows soft (not quite fully extended) raise both arms up until they meet just above your chest, then pass the ball from your left hand to your right hand.

c. With the ball now in your right hand, slowly lower both arms back toward the floor. As soon as your right elbow taps the floor, raise your arms back up to repeat the move in reverse. *Pass the ball back and forth for 1 minute (about 15 reps).*

bathing suit boot **camp!**

Drop and give us 20. Just kidding! But these six moves will help you look and feel great in your suit in just 30 minutes a day. No drill sergeant required!

Certified trainer Elizabeth "Story" Maley, who teaches "Bikini Boot Camp" classes at Crunch Gym in New York City, designed this two-for-one workout that tones your body and burns calories with cardio. She says the reason it's so effective is that you do all the moves standing up (even the ab one), so your heart rate stays elevated throughout the entire workout. Do all six moves two times in a row (it should take about 30 minutes total) and you'll look more toned in about four weeks!

squat lunge

a.

b.

tones: butt and backs of thighs
a. Stand so your left foot's about a foot in front of your right and hold a beach ball a foot in front of your waist.
b. Bend down and touch the ball to the ground about 4 inches in front of your left foot without letting your right knee touch the ground. As you bend, press your left heel into the ground and don't let your left knee come more than an inch over your left toes. (You should feel the muscles in your butt and the back of your left thigh contracting.) Hold the lunge for five seconds, then push off your left heel to stand back up. *Do 2 sets of 10 with your left foot forward, then switch sides and do 2 sets of 10 with your right foot forward.*
CG! tip: If you don't have a beach ball, substitute a roll of paper towels held lengthwise.

rope hops

a.

b.

cardio: tones: butt and thighs

a. Stand with your feet shoulder-width apart and your knees slightly bent about 6 inches to the right of a jump rope (or long piece of string) laid vertically on the ground.

b. Jump back and forth over the rope as quickly as you can, landing about 6 inches away from the rope each time. Be sure to land with your knees soft, not locked. *Jump back and forth for two minutes.*

side stretch

stretches: shoulders, arms, back

a. Holding a beach ball, cross your left foot in front of your right, extend your arms over your head, and lean about a foot to the left. *Hold for 10 seconds.*

b. Switch feet and repeat the stretch on your other side.

no!

no! Don't hunch your shoulders or reach your arms forward (keep them next to your ears); resist bending forward from your waist as you lean.

a.

b.

arm raises

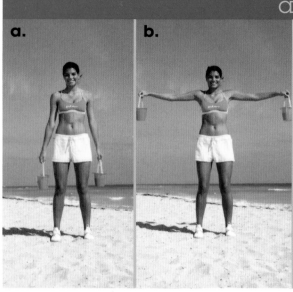

tones: upper arms and shoulders

a. Stand with your feet shoulder-width apart and your arms at your sides, holding two small buckets filled with sand. (Or you can hold two 5-pound dumbbells or two tote bags, each containing two pairs of shoes.)
b. Keep your arms straight without locking your elbows and slowly raise the buckets until your arms are parallel to the ground, then slowly lower them back to your sides. As you raise your arms, keep your wrists strong so they're even with your arms (don't let them go limp), and don't hunch your shoulders toward your ears. *Do 10 arm raises, rest for about 20 seconds, then do another set of 10.*

ab toner

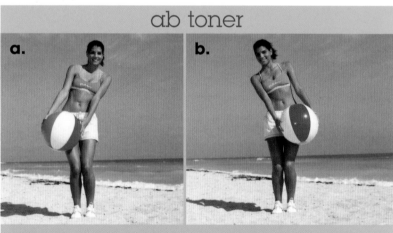

tones: obliques and abs

a. Holding a beach ball in front of you, stand with your feet touching and your inner thighs pressed together. Keeping your lower body still and your abs tight, slowly lean about 8 inches to the left. Keep your arms in line with your shoulders so you're moving the beach ball to your right as you lean to the left. Lean slowly—you should feel your left oblique muscle working. (Even though you do this move standing, it strengthens your abs like a sit-up or crunch would.)
b. Slowly return to the starting position and repeat the move on your right side. *Do 20 reps (10 on each side).*
no! *Don't swing your arms out to the side or bend forward from the waist as you lean.*

no!

rope switches

cardio; tones: calves, thighs, and butt

a. Lay a jump rope in front of you horizontally. (You can also do this move over a piece of string.) Start by standing with your right foot in front of the rope and your left foot behind it.
b. Jump and switch your legs while in midair so that you land with your left foot in front of the rope and your right foot behind it. Each time you land, your feet should be about a foot apart. *Switch back and forth as quickly as you can over the rope for two minutes.* Return to the beginning of the workout and repeat each move one more time.

look great in your **jeans!**

This workout tones the muscles in your lower half and makes your bottom more bootylicious!

To look even better in your favorite basic (jeans!), try this workout from *The Little Butt & Thighs Workout Book,* by Erika Dillman. Each move tones your butt and one other spot, like your thighs, hips, or waist. Do the moves every other day, plus 30 minutes of cardio (like biking) five times a week. You'll begin to notice your jeans fit better.

bent-knee crossover

a.

b.

c.

d.

tones: butt and thighs

a. Kneel on all fours with your hands under your shoulders and knees under hips, with your abs pulled up and in toward your spine.

b. Bend your right leg at a 90-degree angle and slowly lift it until your thigh is parallel to the floor.

c. Keeping your right leg bent, slowly lower right knee to the outside of left leg. It's okay if your knee doesn't touch the floor.

d. Raise right leg back across left, straightening it as you raise it, until leg is extended behind your butt, parallel to floor. Pause, then return to starting position. *Do 3 sets of 8 reps on each.*

standing oblique twist

a.

b.

tones: waist

a. Stand with your feet hip-width apart. Raise your arms so that they're parallel to the floor, then bend your elbows at 90-degree angles so that your hands are above your elbows.

b. Pull your abs up and in toward your spine and slowly rotate your torso to the right while raising your left knee until your thigh is parallel with the floor and your right elbow is above (but not touching) your left knee. Slowly rotate back to the starting position as you lower your leg. Repeat the move on the other side to complete 1 rep. *Do 3 sets of 12 reps.*

single-leg squat

tones: butt and thighs

a. With your arms extended forward (parallel to each other and to the floor), stand on a block 12–15 inches high or on the bottom step of a staircase so that your left side faces the stairs. Put your weight on your left foot and suspend your right foot above the floor in front of the stairs.

b. Keeping your right leg straight, sink your weight into your left heel and lower your butt slightly, as if you were about to sit down (your foot shouldn't touch the floor). Slowly return to the starting position. *Do 3 sets of 8 reps, then switch sides.*

no!

no! Don't allow your bent knee to extend past your toes.

one-legged bridge

tones: butt and hips

a. Lie on your back with your knees bent and your heels about a foot in front of your butt, with your arms at your sides, palms down. Raise your right knee toward your chest.

b. Pull your abs up and in toward your spine and squeeze your butt muscles as you slowly raise your pelvis toward the ceiling until your left knee, hip, and shoulder form a straight line. Pause for two seconds, then, using your butt muscles, slowly lower your pelvis toward the floor, keeping your right knee raised. *Do 3 sets of 8–10 reps, then switch sides.*

jean genie

Your wish for flattering jeans is CosmoGIRL!'s command!

- Wear mid- or low-rise jeans that have a rise of 8–10 inches from the top of the inseam to the waistband, rather than ultra-low-rise jeans, which can make your legs appear shorter.

- Jeans with a uniform medium-to-dark rinse (instead of whiskered, bleached, or faded spots) make your legs look longer.

- Choose jeans with medium-sized back pockets placed on your butt or slightly above it. They draw the eye upward, giving your bum a visual lift.

your
workout
journal

date:

activity:

time/speed/distance/reps:

how i feel today:

notes

date:

activity:

time/speed/distance/reps:

how i feel today:

notes

date:

activity:

time/speed/distance/reps:

how i feel today:

notes

date:

activity:

time/speed/distance/reps:

how i feel today:

notes

126

date:

activity:

time/speed/distance/reps:

how i feel today:

notes